REVIEW IS INSIDE LAST PAGE

NO
bull

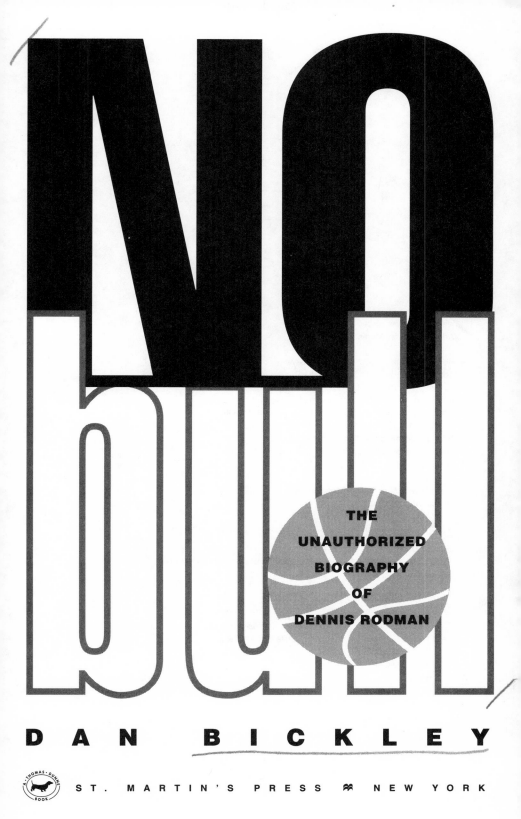

THE
UNAUTHORIZED
BIOGRAPHY
OF
DENNIS RODMAN

DAN BICKLEY

A THOMAS DUNNE BOOK

ST. MARTIN'S PRESS ❦ NEW YORK

A THOMAS DUNNE BOOK.
An imprint of St. Martin's Press

Production Editor: David Stanford Burr
Design by Songhee Kim

        Library of Congress Cataloging-in-Publication Data

Bickley, Dan.
    No Bull : the unauthorized biography of Dennis Rodman / Dan
Bickley.
        p.   cm.
    "A Thomas Dunne book."
    ISBN 0-312-17119-6
    1. Rodman, Dennis, 1961–   . 2. Basketball players—United
States—Biography. 3. Chicago Bulls (Basketball team) I. Title.
GV884.R618B53   1997
796.323'092—dc21
[B]   97-17046
                                       CIP

First Edition: October 1997

10 9 8 7 6 5 4 3 2 1

PERSONAL STUFF

TO ED BICKLEY: Your spirit lives on.

TO THE CHICAGO *SUN-TIMES*: Particularly Nigel Wade,
Bill Adee, Phil Rosenthal, and Jay Mariotti.
Thanks for the support and encouragement.

TO TAMI BARTLETT: For everything

CONTENTS

FOREWORD

Favorite meal: Soup and Sugar Bears.
ESPN Biofile of Dennis Rodman

There is plenty of room at the end of the century for an antihero, and here he is, sprawling on a bed in the suite of a Chicago hotel.

Two of his bodyguards mill about in the back corner of the expansive room, waiting for the evening to begin. Soon there will be drinks to consume, women to select, and a crush of adoring fans besieging their employer the moment he decides to feed his nocturnal rage. The adrenaline is building.

A public relations flack tells the antihero to concentrate, for there are only a few more interviews left before he can return to his sandbox of hedonism.

He is undoubtedly bored, staring at the television through a pair of sunglasses, offering not a hint of emotion.

We see only what he wants us to see, and his must be a life of high maintenance, especially on days like these.

And then Dennis Rodman lets us in on a little secret:

"I don't need to fool around with you," he says. "I don't have to.

"It's very easy to fool the media. Very easy. Very easy to manipulate them. You've never seen anyone act or do some of the things I've done in sports."

Indeed, there has never been an athlete who has captivated the sporting world quite like Dennis Rodman.

He is from a generation of sweat and inspiration, playing a game of finesse with reckless abandon. He is the prima donna's worst nightmare, and in his profession, no one works harder.

He never played high school basketball, but after an amazing growth spurt near his twentieth birthday, he became a small-college superstar. And buoyed by unbridled enthusiasm and endless energy, he found a niche in the NBA.

In the past eight years, he has redefined the art of rebounding, perfecting and popularizing a craft not seen since the days of Wes Unseld and Paul Silas. And no one his size has ever been more productive in his area of expertise.

He is gifted with the greatest pair of legs in NBA history, tree-trunk thighs attached to a slender frame, yielding an explosive combination of agility, speed, and power.

He is a proven winner, owner of four championship rings and counting. He has been part of only one losing season in his career, and is one of the most productive playoff performers the game has ever seen.

And that's only half the story.

He has become the master of self-promotion, a showman with the strangest appeal. He is the cross-dressing male lauded for his sense of style, yet voted the worst-dressed woman in an annual survey. He changes his hair color like a chameleon, and flaunts his individuality with contempt.

He is the car wreck that makes us shudder, yet compels us to stop and look. And now he has shrewdly crossed over the boundaries of athletics and into the realm of entertainment.

He has starred in one motion picture, and is plotting a further invasion of Hollywood. He has recorded a song, marketed a line of dolls and lollipops, and flooded bookstores with two autobiographies in the past year.

"You can't get away from him," said Bob Hill, Rodman's former coach with the San Antonio Spurs. "He's created this image, and everything he does, we wonder if he did it on purpose. But he's broken through and gotten beyond the ridiculous.

"I was with a few friends at a bar, and the minute I mentioned 'Dennis Rodman' they sat up on the edge of their chairs. What other athlete has that kind of effect?"

Yet Dennis Rodman is also cursed with an uncontrollable temper, one that surfaces in tremors, always leading to the inevitable quake that tears down the walls. He has caused coaches to buckle at his feet, general managers to panic in apprehension, and forced chaotic upheaval in every organization that has employed his services.

He has been suspended ten times since 1992, three times for head-butting either a referee or an opposing player, once for kicking a courtside cameraman.

He is prisoner to impulsive behavior, and must constantly feel like a martyr, even if it means creating his own punishment.

He is despised by opponents who are prone to his cheap shots and dirty tricks. He is the scourge of all referees, who endure his boorish act on a nightly basis.

Dennis Rodman is a self-made player.

And he is a self-made mystery.

He is in love with his alter ego, which he nurtures with calculated care, covers with makeup, and sells to the fringes of a society drawn to the tent of freaks. And operating on the periphery of the great circus, he is masterful, confident, in control.

But in the soft moments, he is a man-child lost in suspended adolescence, fortified by a small circle of eclectic friends. During basketball season, he lives in a modest ranch home in the Chicago suburbs, and his living room is sparse, holding only a sixty-inch television set and a mattress.

There is no need for much else. Rodman spends his mornings at practice, his afternoons in the weight room, and his evenings at a few Chicago nightclubs like Crobar, Elbo Room, and the Smart Bar. He plays hard, on and off the court, and sleeps when he collapses, which is often near sunrise.

He is the great paradox, straddling the psychological borders of incredible complexity and unnerving simplicity.

"Dennis is obviously a person of dual personalities," Bulls coach Phil Jackson said.

Deserving or not, Rodman has also become the symbol of rebellious, petulant youth, tapping into the I-don't-give-a-fuck attitude that somehow fills an enormous hole that has opened in the marketplace. He is a glaring alternative to the Milquetoast, "wholesome" athlete who represents values no longer salient in a nation bored with its bland array of heroes.

He is the champion of narcissism, the voice of liberation, the master of self-expression in an era of bad manners. He is the exhibitionist dripping with sexuality, a James Dean on steroids, and his appearance makes females squirm with desire and men shake their heads in complete role confusion.

He is hailed as the torch-bearer for gender hopping, an athlete who has broken through the restrictive locker room of moral subservience. He is the statue of indifference, and whether you love him or loathe him, he simply doesn't care.

And, boy, how cool is that?

Piece together the sound bites, the suspensions, the angry defiance, and the friend who saw him pick up six women at a bar without saying a word, and you understand his enormous popularity: he is the epicenter of a decadent orgy, creator of a highly restricted club where inhibitions are checked at the door. And we are all outside, clamoring in line for a peek, desperate for the privilege of membership.

In the homogenous diet of conformity, he is a big bag of Sugar Bears.

"People love me because I'm unique," Rodman said. "People love me because I'm what you all would be if you could let it all hang out."

But where do perception and reality intersect in this wild portrait? And do we really want to know?

What is a man who worships at the altar of selfishness, servant to his own desires? Is he beyond shrewd, the rare entertainer who recognizes and fills a void before we even know it exists? Or is he as baffled by his own staggering rise to fame as we are?

Is he legitimate? Or the ultimate con man, peddling a store full of hypocrisy to loyal patrons blinded by illusion?

"I fuck with people's minds," Rodman said. "You've never met anyone like me. I'm not afraid of anything. I'm up for every challenge. I can take a punch, and so far, so good. I'm still standing.

"No matter how hard people try to knock me down, I always seem to be one step ahead. And that's what keeps me being successful. That's my strength, staying focused, visualizing the next step in the adventure and not being afraid to do it."

No doubt, Dennis Rodman has spent the last decade screaming for attention. From a tattoed body resembling a walking billboard to the Crayola box of hair colors, he is begging to be noticed. So is his soul filled with an undeniable strength of spirit so easily romanticized, or is he simply overcompensating for a childhood of painful anonymity?

Even at night, he is rarely seen without sunglasses, avoiding eye contact at all costs. Those who know him swear that he is remarkably intelligent, but he also has a terrible time with verbal expression.

Is he really secure as steel, completely detached from the need for approbation? Or is the gauge of self-esteem continually on empty, hidden under the sequined dress?

"One thing I know for sure about Dennis is that, as much as he tries to act like he doesn't care, he needs to be accepted and loved," said Glenn "Doc" Rivers, a former teammate in the NBA. "He hates to be disliked."

Indeed, those who have forged even surface relationships with Rodman see through the disguise. His "bad boy" image is both necessary and convenient, providing Rodman with a fortress of armor he could never find on the elusive road to manhood.

But for the most part, it is a façade.

"Most people only know him in terms of what they see," said former teammate Isiah Thomas. "But there is a beautiful person inside the Dennis Rodman that only a few people know. Only people very close to him get a chance to see that."

I have spent a good part of the past two years in the presence of Dennis Rodman and witnessed up close the different facets of his personality. I have tried to penetrate his unbearable shyness, gawked at his explosive tantrums, and shaken my head in disbelief over his ability to garner attention.

I have chatted with a seven-year-old boy who attended a Bulls game in drag, complete with lipstick, makeup, and a feather boa in hopes of earning Rodman's attention. He did.

I have held his can of beer in the hallway of the United Center while he signed autographs for a legion of normally sane females. And I have witnessed his incredible magnetism when he hits the streets at night.

In the course of covering professional sports for the past ten years, I have seen the potent lure athletes have for the opposite sex. But I have never seen anyone tap into the female libido quite like Dennis Rodman.

I have seen him take the stage as a surprise guest at a Stone Temple Pilots concert, singing the encore with the band. When I asked him if he was nervous, he pointed to his sunglasses, telling me he couldn't see a thing.

But for me, the most poignant and telling moment happened during the 1996 playoffs, when I was scrambling to listen in on Rodman's moving press conference. Walking behind him at a frantic pace, I stepped on Rodman's shoe, dislodging it from his foot. A flat tire, as they call it in grammar school.

Rodman spun around, and instead of flashing the expected scowl, he broke into a grin that spoke volumes of his penchant for fifth-grade fun.

That, in my opinion, is the real Dennis Rodman.

For while he mingles in an elite stratosphere, dating Madonna, posing in *Playboy*, and vacationing with Eddie Vedder, there is an endearing, layman quality to Rodman that makes him nearly impossible to dislike.

He is Peter Pan in basketball shorts, and his innocence can melt your preconceptions in a heartbeat. It is a trait easily spotted in the eyes of children, who gravitate to Rodman as if he were the pied piper.

"That's because Dennis is like a kid," said his mother. Shirley. "I'm not sure what age he'd be now, but I'd say he's gotten up to fifteen."

Beneath all the bluster, Rodman is also generous to a fault, and in every city where he has played basketball, there are numerous stories of how he'll stop at a red light, roll down the window of his truck, and hand a fistful of money to the homeless.

It has happened in Detroit, San Antonio, and Chicago. It happens everywhere, and there are witnesses to prove it.

"I take few things seriously," Rodman said. "I don't take life too seriously. But I take people that are not fortunate very seriously. *Very* seriously."

Consider his self-destructive behavior: he once burrowed himself into a Las Vegas hotel for a month and lost $35,000, and he was teetering near the edge of bankruptcy in 1995. There are those who think Rodman has a death wish—that he doesn't feel he deserves the wealth he attains, and in an attempt to rid himself of the anxiety, just gives it all back.

But more to the point, it is a reflection of Rodman's own self-image. If it weren't for one growth spurt, that would be him begging on the corner, shivering in the cold and sleeping on the pavement.

"What Dennis does for the needy is the side that nobody ever sees," said Brendan Suhr, a former assistant coach for the Detroit Pistons. "Whether it be the homeless guy that he brings home for dinner or how he used to spend Thanksgiving feeding people at a mission in Detroit, he has an amazing source of compassion. And it's because he's been there."

So strip away the layers of eccentricity, and at heart, he is the Soup, the common man removed from a common existence by a single genetic explosion. And to forget the lunchbox population would be to forget the only part of himself that is real, a blue-collar work ethic that is the only logical reason he can find for his success.

"Dennis cares," Michael Jordan said. "He may project an I-don't-care attitude, but he is very sensitive to how he is perceived. You can see right through that shield he puts up because of his shyness and the misunderstanding that surrounds him."

Along the way, he has picked up the accessories that now define Rodmania, a challenge that gets tougher and tougher as our cultural barometer becomes more and more callous. It is very possible that he spends most of his waking hours wondering how he is being perceived and what must be unveiled next, consumed with what people are thinking of Dennis Rodman.

It's also likely that Rodman doesn't understand the phenomenon himself, simply feasting on the attention until he's full, putting down his plate, and waiting until the pang in his soul resurfaces.

Last year, during the Bulls' glorious playoff run, Rodman walked into a restaurant after a game and found his former coach and mentor, Chuck Daly, sitting at a table.

Daly couldn't hide his curiosity. He wanted to know what had sparked such a notorious change in Rodman, a player so introverted that he'd go weeks without saying a word to his teammates.

"He said to me, 'I spent all those years in Detroit, I was Defensive Player of the Year, I was an All-Star, I led the league in rebounding, and nobody knew who I was and I certainly wasn't getting paid the way I should. Coach, I had to find another way,' " Daly said. "He found out he could tweak the NBA, its administrators, and the entire world by acting outrageous."

So it's all an act?

"Absolutely," Daly said. "He's taken it to the nth degree, and he'll never look better than he did in that bridal dress."

So who is Dennis Rodman? A complex mystery? Or a figment of our imagination?

He is still sprawling on the bed, and the volume of the television in the hotel suite has been turned up. There is a cartoon holding his attention, but he understands the question.

"Once I die, you can take all the things they write about me, put 'em all together, and now you'll have the real Dennis Rodman," he said. "You'll never see the Dennis Rodman, the real individual, until the day he dies.

"People are slowly and surely trying to figure out what's going on with Dennis Rodman, who he really is, what he really wants to be. I can't say what's misunderstood. Whatever you write, whatever you think, that's what you believe."

Indeed, and the answer is either a lucky guess or pure genius.

Because it's very possible that he lives only in the quirky closet of our consciousness, and to strip him to the core might be a hollow journey.

For what we think about Dennis Rodman probably says more about us than it does about him.

one

"He always believed that Daddy was

coming back."

Shirley Rodman, Dennis's mother

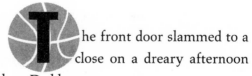he front door slammed to a close on a dreary afternoon in February, and just like that, Daddy was gone.

Off to McGuire Air Force Base for mandatory field maneuvers.

Out of your life forever.

Of course, you didn't know at the time. You were only three and one half years old, and the last thing you remember is a somewhat joyous trip to the ice cream parlor earlier that day. And as far as you can tell, everything seemed, well, normal.

But the moment he leaves for work, your mother jumps into action, pulling out suitcases and stuffing them full of clothes. She is fiercely determined, and you sense the urgency, that something serious is going down. She calls you and your sisters into the living room, and you learn you're going back to Texas. Again.

But your mother vows that this time will be permanent, and once the ordeal is over, she will never move again.

You stare at your mother, unable to comprehend the magnitude of her decision. But like it or not, there is a train waiting in nearby Trenton, and you must immediately leave your home and your father in Wrightstown, New Jersey.

You ride deep into the night, stopping to switch trains in St. Louis. And then you're off to Dallas, where your mother will wipe the slate clean and start all over again.

But what about you? Where do you put the pain? And how do you deal with such utter abandonment?

All that drives Dennis Rodman—his desperate need for attention, a persecution complex that surfaces whenever he is singled out for punishment, a withdrawn personality that disappears only when the camera turns on—can be easily traced to a disoriented childhood.

How much of his behavior can be attributed to an upbringing skewed by embarrassment and fear is unknown, for every childhood is a journey through insecurity and trauma. But it's safe to say that Rodman had more than his share.

"Not a lot of happy moments," Rodman said. "I didn't have much."

He didn't have his father, a man who broke the sacred vows of marriage—though infidelity means nothing to a child barely old enough to walk.

He didn't have strength of self, enduring the ridicule of classmates who preyed on a meek and easy target, a child too passive to fight back.

He didn't have a shred of ambition, prompting his mother to finally open the door and send an apathetic, unmotivated teenager into the streets.

He was a child who matured slowly, a momma's boy forced to retreat into the safety of a household dominated by females, a troubled adolescent who chose not to grow up, draining the patience of the only parent he's ever known.

This is the story of Dennis Rodman, the fragmented foundation underneath the strangest house on the block.

"I don't think Dennis was an unhappy child," said his mother, Shirley Rodman. "I just think he was a child who never had a father. And when I was cast into the role of a single parent, I was no more prepared than anyone else. I didn't know a thing about raising children."

Indeed, Shirley was a sheltered girl from a large family. Her father died when she was five, and she was raised by the firm hand of her mother and an extended support group. She had never left the state of Texas, and was making her way through junior college when she met Philander Rodman, Jr., in 1960.

He was everything she wasn't—a worldly romantic, enlisted in the United States Air Force. And he knocked her off her feet.

Literally.

Their first introduction was by collision at a local skating rink, and three months later they were married. Philander was subsequently assigned to a military base in New Jersey, and Shirley was immediately pried from the only comfort zone she had ever known. They had three children in rapid succession—Dennis, Debra, and Kim—all one year apart in age.

Early in the marriage, Philander developed a taste for adultery, and his appetite continued to grow. And when his side dishes began calling Shirley at home and asking for her husband, well, her shroud of naïveté quickly dissolved.

"I couldn't take it," she said. "It was just devastating to find out what kind of person I married. I just didn't know anything. I didn't have any street smarts. I believed in the sanctity of marriage, that it was a commitment that lasted forever. I didn't know anything about reality outside the home. But he just was not a very good husband."

Twice she took her anger and her children back to Dallas. Twice she was conned by the words of her husband. Twice she returned to New Jersey, believing that Philander had finally changed.

But on that fateful afternoon in 1965, when her courage had been fortified by endless shame, Shirley Rodman had seen enough. At the age of twenty-five, with a scarred heart and zero job experience, she moved back home to Dallas, back under the roof of her mother. For the next four months, she was too humiliated, too humbled and too shattered to leave the house.

Eventually, after agreeing upon a divorce with Philander, she climbed back on her feet. And when she did, Shirley Rodman made a vow to be self-sufficient, and never to lose her dignity again.

"I had never worked a day in my life, but I wanted to support them, to give them a life without depending on welfare," she said. "I didn't know what I was doing, but you can't just throw up both hands and say, 'I give up.' "

Shirley tried to work with the government to attain child support under Philander's military coverage, but claims she was shut out of all benefits. So she held as many as four jobs at once to keep her family solvent—working as a church musician, a bus driver, a merchandise checker at an assembly line, and a grade-school teacher. She went back to school, taking classes in the evening, eventually earning three different associate degrees.

She wore a mask of fierce independence until it became real. She enrolled her children in as many after-school activities as she could find. She became a disciplinarian, afraid to let her guard down in front of her children.

"Coming in tired at night, the times when I was most vulnerable, I never let my children see that," Shirley said. "I fought it the best way I knew how. But when you only see your children late at night and eary in the morning, when you work the hours I had to, something is going to suffer in the process. Something is going to give."

"I couldn't give my children all the things they wanted. But I was always brutally honest."

Shirley Rodman

Admittedly, she didn't have the time or the energy to shower her children with love, and besides, that would only feed a flowery perception that had blown up in her face. It didn't seem to affect her daughters, who were sprouting strong branches of independence and self-confidence. But inside, Shirley began to worry about Dennis's suppressed development.

In all the after-school programs, Dennis was perceived as the baby of the family, even though he was the oldest. He was alarmingly shy and introverted. He would say as little as possible, preferring to cling to his mother's leg.

"He always wanted to be under me," Shirley said.

"When it comes to stuff like that, it's more of a fog to me. It's just a figment of my imagination."

Dennis Rodman, on his early childhood

In elementary school, Dennis developed fierce allergies and nasty facial sores, causing him to withdraw even further. In retrospect, Shirley says she mishandled the subject of her ex-husband.

Instead of laying the facts on Dennis at a young age, she allowed him to idealize the vision of his father, even to the point where he was convinced that his dad was coming back. This smothering of truth caused Dennis a bundle of internal stress, which she attributed to his physical maladies.

"I had the tendency not to let my kids see everything that was hard," she said. "We were always living in an area that was not the best. We weren't living in the projects, like I keep hearing. It was fixed-income housing, and we had a nice apartment.

"But I just thought the less they knew about their father and his activities, the less they would hate him. In all their eyes, we were just separated. That was not good for us, but I didn't know any better. I just always believed he would eventually contact the children, but he never did. And to be perfectly honest, with all the hours I was working, he was the last thing on my mind."

Yet she knew Dennis was short on self-esteem, and needed a male role model in the worst way. He was skinny and frail, a "very sickly" child. He had few friends, preferring to hang around his sisters, who were developing quickly and beginning to excel in athletics.

Although carefree in the company of his sisters. Dennis was taunted by classmates in school, some of whom physically threatened Rodman to get him to hand over his lunch money.

In order to comply, to blend in without making waves, Dennis began stealing from his mother to pay off his enemies.

"Dennis doesn't like to hurt people's feelings," she said. "And they'd hurt his a million times. He'd give in to things that he didn't really want to do. So I had to be overly protective. There were kids in school that were just brutalizing Dennis. I jumped on that right away."

Upon learning of her son's troubles at school, Shirley transferred Dennis to another school, soothing her son's fears, if only temporarily.

Constantly overshadowed by his sisters, Rodman would follow them to the local recreation center to play basketball. He had long arms and could run like the wind, and even at a tender age showed a certain prowess as a rebounder. But while his sisters were the picture of grace, he was gangly and awkward.

When Dennis entered South Oak Cliff High School, he finally summoned the will to strike out on his own. As a freshman, he tried out for the football team. And while the coaches marveled at his speed, they deemed him simply too small to survive in such a rough sport.

He was cut. He was devastated. And once again, Shirley was forced into the fray.

She demanded a meeting with the coach who had cut Dennis during tryouts.

"I'm sorry, but he's too small," the coach said.

Undaunted, Shirley accompanied Dennis to school one day, and demanded another meeting.

Same answer. And while Dennis seemed fine on the outside, shrugging off the setback with an indifference that would become his trademark, he was torn up inside.

"I interfered in my children's lives quite a bit," Shirley said. "I refused to believe that I couldn't do that. I knew Dennis was upset, but Dennis was the type of boy to keep everything inside. I don't think any parent really knows the inside of anyone's mind, but I do know that Dennis didn't reveal a lot of the things he was feeling."

Later that year, Dennis made the basketball team. But for all his eagerness, his skills were unpolished and raw. He was relegated to the bench, and midway through the season, he quit.

Shirley tried to find something to coax Dennis out of his shell, but nothing worked.

Her concern deepened.

"The poor little thing . . . he was only about five-foot-six for the longest time," she said. "The girls, they just shot up past him. We didn't try to make him feel like a weakling, but he just got overwhelmed.

"There was nothing but girls in the house. They shot up past him, and he was sickly all the time."
Shirley Rodman

"All throughout high school, all he wanted to do was hang with the girls. And when they would go to their [basketball] games, he'd just stay in his room and play video games. . . . He didn't go out very much."

Shirley tried everything she could to steer Dennis out of his shell. She contacted the Big Brother Association, an organization designed to help single parents, particularly single mothers. The association paired Dennis with a man she knows only as "Mr. Haynes," who would take Dennis to football games and other functions. And while she remembers him as a "very kind man," he made no noticeable impact on her son.

In a stunning statement, Rodman now claims he is dealing with repressed memories of being sexually abused by a male when he was younger. In an interview with *The Advocate*, a national gay and lesbian news magazine, Rodman claims he is convinced that somewhere in his past he was forced to have sex with another man.

"I feel like I was going through a change in my life for some reason," he told the magazine. "I couldn't take time with no man. I was afraid to be around boys my age. I was afraid of being around guys.

"I thought guys would make fun of me. So I was hanging around my mother and sisters, and I felt like I was a girl. And for some reason I keep flashing back and thinking that I had sex with a man when I was young.

"Yeah, I think that I've had sex with a man. It keeps coming back to me."

He is then asked by the interviewer if he was a teenager at the time.

"Yeah," Rodman said. "I swear to God. It's so real that every time it pops up I try to dig deeper and deeper. Did it really happen?"

He is asked if he's undergone therapy to help uncover the mystery.

"I have, but I don't think therapy can help me. I think I have to do it myself. I think I'm strong enough and mentally able to do it myself because I practice visualization, and for some reason I think I've had sex with a man. Not on my terms.

"Not by my father, by somebody else. [My father] was long gone. I think that I was—and I've never told anybody this—abused when I was younger by a man."

When Shirley Rodman was told of her son's revelation, she burst into laughter.

"He does know how to make money, doesn't he?" she said. "As far as my mind can take me, I never had a man in the house after his father left us. It just wasn't my style.

"The only man around was Mr. Haynes, who was only allowed to come during daylight hours. He was a decent man, he never would've done that.

"I have stated in the past that men were just not a factor when it came to my children. I just didn't have them around. As a parent, you don't know everything that your children do, but I know for a fact that Dennis was never sexually abused. I think he just said that to impress whoever he was talking to."

Rodman also states that his mother found him a Big Brother because she was worried that he might be gay. She says this, too, is absurd.

"I just knew he needed a male influence," she said.

"I didn't know what was going on. I was scared. My mother wouldn't hire me a big brother so I could be around men. I think she thought that something was seriously going on there. Mothers have those instincts."

Dennis Rodman in *The Advocate*

By 1979, Dennis's senior year in high school, he had grown to five feet nine inches. He had traded in his clinging nature for a detached cool, knowing he had to break away somehow. He discovered a few new friends, and began finding fun in the strangest places.

If he wasn't breaking into school during off hours for a cheap thrill, he was navigating a nasty underground sewer system that led to the state fairgrounds. The latter remains one of Dennis's most vivid memories of childhood.

While Dennis worked his share of odd jobs, the first as a busboy at Baby Doe's restaurant in Dallas, he had no direction whatsoever—in striking contrast to his sisters, who were loaded with ambition. Both were big-time basketball prospects, and for Debra and Kim, the future was structured and smooth. Debra, who stood six feet two and specialized in defense and rebounding, would earn a college scholarship to Louisiana Tech, a perennial power in women's basketball. Kim, two inches shorter, was successfully courted by Stephen F. Austin.

"I was beginning to get a little antsy about Dennis," Shirley said. "I was beginning to worry about him constantly. I wanted him to pull away from me. I used everybody I could. I was determined that Dennis was going to get out of the house.

"He was eighteen, and he had never dated a girl in his life. I don't know if it was my influence or the girls', but he just wasn't growing up."

As Shirley's determination strengthened, her relationship with Dennis became tense. She married again, much to her son's disapproval. She would find evidence that he was once again stealing from her purse, but this time, there was no logical reason, no bullies scaring the daylights out of Dennis at school.

The second marriage didn't last long, but Dennis's apathy only worsened. He had no desire to go to college, and began hanging out with older men at the recreation center.

He worked long enough to keep his pockets full of change until he scored a job that he thought would be his permanent vocation— earning $6.50 per hour as overnight janitor at the Dallas–Fort Worth airport.

"He just threw up his hands," Shirley said. "He decided he'd be a janitor for the rest of his life. I tried to tell Dennis that there was more to life than what was going on inside my house. I knew, in his heart, that he wanted to play basketball.

"But all his life, he kept getting rejected because he was sickly and little and puny. Everyone would always bypass him for someone who was stronger and bigger. It knocked his self-esteem to the lowest point, and there was no getting up.

"I don't think the children loved me. They depended on me."

Shirley Rodman

"It sounds like a story that needs violins, doesn't it?"

two

FREEZE FRAMED

"The actor reached through an expandable gate covering the entrance to the store and removed sixteen (16) watches valued at $470."
Airport security case report

The sun had barely risen over the rough edges of Dallas, and the actor was buried in his room, lost in a deep sleep.

He was unaware of the suspicious vehicle that had navigated through the forgotten blocks of low-income housing, turning intently onto Sunnyvale Drive, stopping on the curb outside apartment #144. And he was oblivious to the ominous knocking at the front door, a strange occurrence for eight o'clock on a summer morning in the projects.

But it was a heavy and insistent pounding, the kind that just sounds like trouble, and Shirley Rodman ambled to the door.

Outside, she found two white detectives—sergeants Jerry Ellison and Don Adams—holding an arrest warrant.

They were looking for Dennis Keith Rodman.

As in any low-income, predominantly black area existing in the shadows of a big city, the residents of Oak Cliff learned to be leery of the police, especially when they're white and looking for your son.

Shirley Rodman held her ground.

"Why? What did he do?" she insisted.

One of the detectives pulled a watch from his pocket, one nearly identical to the model Dennis had given his mother a few weeks ago.

"Come on in," Shirley said.

Over a month earlier, Dennis Keith Rodman had shown up for work at the Dallas–Fort Worth airport. He had just landed a job as overnight custodian, and on July 28, he was doing his rounds in the Braniff Terminal.

He stopped in front of the Aeroplex gift shop at Gate 20 and glanced around, making sure he hadn't missed any supervisors or nosy tourists lingering in the vicinity. But it was after 1:00 A.M., and the airport was empty.

He was carrying a long stick equpped with a hook on the end, and extended it through the security gates of a dark shop. He knew that a bounty of watches were removed from the display case at the close of business and hidden behind the counter. And like a bear plucking helpless salmon out of a shallow stream, he began fishing watches out of the store, one by one, until his pockets were full.

Rodman heisted sixteen watches that morning, some costing as much as $70, robbing the store of $470 worth of merchandise. He had been fingered by two of his younger friends, who also worked at the airport and were found wearing Timex watches matching the description of the stolen goods.

And when Melvin Michael Jones, twelve, and Benny VonDrake Jones, fourteen, said their friend Dennis had sold them the watches for ten dollars apiece, the trail led to Shirley Rodman's door.

So on August 30, 1979, Dennis Rodman was busted. He was awakened by his mother, staggered out of his room in his undershorts, and found a pair of handcuffs waiting for breakfast.

He was escorted to the airport jail, a small holding facility, and thrown into a cell with another man charged with illegally boarding an airplane.

He was eighteen years old, and scared out of his wits. Outside the steady wrath of his mother, he had never been in trouble before. He was stunned by how serious his crime was being perceived, and the ramifications gave birth to a lump in his throat.

He was asked to give a statement, and his brain whirred, searching for a plausible explanation.

I had been working for BIC Guardian Maintenance for about five days. Night shift. Melvin and Benny Jones said, "Come on, let's get some watches." I went with them to the gift shop at Gate 20. It was about one something in the morning and the shop was closed. A metal gate was locked across the front. The Jones boys got a bunch of watches with a stick with a hook on it. I reached through the gate with my hand and got two watches. One was a silver Timex with a leather band. The other one was a gold Timex with a leather band. I threw the boxes in the trash and put one of the watches on my arm and the other one in my pocket. I took them home with me, and the next day, I gave them away.

Rodman spent one terrifying, lonely night in jail—the edict of his mother, who thought her son was a slumbering through life, desperately in need of a jarring wake-up call. This was just fine with the authorities as well, for not only did they have a petty thief in their possession, but one who refused to come clean. They knew Rodman had stolen more than two watches.

And later the next day, they laid out the truth about their adolescent prisoner: his thievery had been recorded by a surveillance monitor in the gift shop, his cunning and daring heist caught on tape.

It would be the last time that Dennis Rodman was ever unaware of a camera in his presence.

three
THE GIFT

"He just had a little bad period."

Shirley Rodman

Shirley Rodman shut the door of her apartment, sat down at the table, and sorted through the confusion.

Her son had just been arrested for burglary, taken off to jail in handcuffs.

Instinctively, she wanted to jump up, find her son, and rescue him from the pain and indignity of prison. But she also wanted to teach him a lesson, and all her previous methods had fallen on deaf ears. It was time for tough love.

"I knew they could only keep him for three days," Shirley said. "But I decided to leave him in there for the whole seventy-two hours."

Predictably, she was overcome with guilt and her resolve melted later that night. She decided to find and free her son the next morning, hoping that a single night in jail would provide a stark lesson in reality. The next morning, Shirley set out to have her son released, but found out he was not in the county jail, as she thought.

"I was racing around all day, trying to make bond," Shirley said. "And he wasn't even downtown [at the county jail]. He was never booked. I found that out, and I wasn't so worried anymore."

Yet the mix-up had forced Dennis to spend another day in prison, and when he was finally released into his mother's custody, his soul was raw with fear, his head numb from tears that couldn't stop flowing.

"He said he was trying to do something nice for other people, that he didn't even keep a single watch for himself," Shirley said. "He had to spend a night down there, and I don't think he felt too good. But I let him know just how stupid it was. And I let him know over and over again."

Rodman's court date was set for September 19, but the charges were dropped before he went to trial. But he was visibly shaken by the incident, and told his mother that the episode would be a turning point in his life.

Another year passed, and Rodman stayed out of jail, shying away from the kind of trouble that could land him back in prison.

But not much changed.

"I was getting a little antsy about Dennis. He was growing up so slowly."
Shirley Rodman

He was almost twenty years old, still lazy and unmotivated, buried in a bedroom as life passed him by. He was impossible to reach, and worse yet, didn't care about much other than playing pinball and hanging with his friends.

And then came the gift, a genetic blessing that changed the course of history.

In a matter of one year, Rodman grew eleven inches.

As if his life were a cartoon, he simply burst out of his old body, his old clothes, and sprouted to the sky. And he never stopped.

He was once a frail five feet nine, a boy whose police alias was listed as "Slim."

He was now six feet eight, a stick figure that stood in the clouds.

"Just like that," Rodman said. "It was like I woke up one day and had a new body."

For a while, it only added to Dennis's confusion. He had grown out of all of his clothes, and for the longest time wore only one outfit, a baggy pair of overalls. He was convinced that he was a freak, that his appearance was even more revolting than the previous model.

"Within two to three weeks, he was growing out of everything," Shirley said. "He'd say, 'Momma, something's wrong. Something's wrong with my body.' He worried so much that he broke out in allergies."

He was still shy, still terribly afraid of failure, still convinced he looked like a dork. But he started playing basketball again at the recreation center, and for the first time in his life, he was dominating.

Norita Westbrook, a family friend who had grown up with Debra and Kim, was home for the summer when she spotted Dennis playing basketball. She was stunned.

"Dennis was always a good basketball player, even when he was much younger," Westbrook said. "But when I came back to the neighborhood and saw how he had grown, it was unbelievable. Now, everyone wanted Dennis on their team.

"I began thinking. The men's program at my school was having a real hard time recruiting. They were looking for guys to play basketball, and I knew Dennis was at home, not doing much of anything."

She went back to her school in Gainesville, Texas, then known as Cooke County Junior College, where she was on scholarship to play basketball. Back on campus, she rushed to find Bill Broom, who was the head women's coach and the assistant men's coach.

"Coach, you're looking for players, right?" she asked.

"Yeah," her coach said. "What do you got?"

"Coach, you remember Dennis Rodman, don't you?"

"Yeah, so what. He can't play."

"Coach, you won't believe this. He's about six foot eight now, and he's been playing in the recreation center. You better go check him out."

Broom immediately jumped on Westbrook's lead. He found Rodman at the recreation center, introduced himself, and brought his new recruit back to the school for a visit.

"I knew the family because I had recruited his sisters," Broom said. "But I knew Dennis hadn't played any basketball in high school. She insisted that I check on him, and finally, I thought, 'What the heck.'

"She was right. He had grown, and he had gotten pretty darn good. And better yet, nobody was recruiting him. We got him up here, talked to him, and signed him up just like that."

Rodman signed on for two years, a full ride for 1982–83 and 1983–84. He had never played organized basketball before, but had little trouble adapting. He was smarter than he acted, and picked up the offensive structure immediately.

He listened attentively and complied with everything the coaching staff asked. He practiced like a mule, unaware of his growing status. He had found an escape hatch from the shadows of his siblings, and it all seemed too good to be true.

In sixteen games for Cooke County, Rodman averaged 17.6 points and 13.3 rebounds per game. He couldn't make a free throw—shooting just 58.2 percent from the foul line—but had a nifty shooting percentage of 61.6 from the field.

"He would do the dirty work, he'd play defense, and he would put in the hours," Broom said. "Say what you want about the guy, but he works hard. And because of that, he really developed quick. We couldn't believe what we had stumbled onto, especially for someone who had never played basketball in high school."

Problem was, Rodman didn't go to class, even though he had taken only three to begin with—the minimum in order to retain athletic eligibility. After one semester, he flunked out.

He told his coaches that he would be back the following semester, that he would begin focusing on his academics.

He was fooling himself, lying to his coaches. He never returned.

"It was like going out and finding a diamond," Broom said. "And just like that, he was gone."

Rodman drifted back home, settling back into a life without pressure. But his mother had reached the breaking point. She wasn't ready for this kind of false start from Dennis, and she began questioning whether his lack of ambition was her fault.

She had done everything possible to nurture her son, to have patience with his shortcomings, to hold his hand through every ordeal. Although Dennis rarely spoke to anyone, she knew he was intelligent. She knew he was wasting his life, and this hurt more than anything.

As she had done with her ex-husband almost two decades before, she smothered all sympathy and took the hard line.

"I got to realizing that I would be supporting this boy the rest of my life," Shirley said. "I told him he had three choices: he could get a job, go back to school, or go into the [military] service. He was just lying around, doing nothing. So I gave him a choice. Either he was going to do one of those three things, or he was going to get out of my house. I needed to find some peace of mind."

Dennis was initially stunned at his mother's outburst, but figured it would blow over in a matter of time.

Two days later, she found Dennis hanging out with his sorry group of friends, and that was it. Shirley Rodman opened the door, and pushed her son into the streets.

"I told Dennis, 'Look, you want to be out there with your friends, go on.'" Shirley said.

"How long does this have to go on? When does the point come when you say, 'Hey, you're on your own'? When does a parent say that? I didn't know. I just knew one thing: I had enough, and something had to be done."

four
GREAT ESCAPE

> **"You put in the hours, you beat the bushes,**
> **and you always keep looking.**
> **Because you never know**
> **what you're going to find."**
> **Lonn Reisman**

onn Reisman pulled into the parking lot at Cooke County Junior College, purchased a ticket for the men's basketball game, and settled into the bleachers.

As an assistant basketball coach and recruiter for Southeastern Oklahoma State, a small NAIA school in Durant, Oklahoma, it was Reisman's job to scour the obscure programs, to find players who had somehow slipped past the omniscient watch of talent evaluators across the country.

It is a tricky job, for all the top-level talent is normally swept away by the glitter and glamour of Division I universities, perennial powers like North Carolina, Duke, and Michigan. But if you search long enough, if you spend enough time in empty, anonymous gymnasiums, you might get lucky and find a kid who developed late or didn't have the grades. And Reisman would be there, offering an option for athletes short on such a commodity.

Just a few months earlier, Reisman had walked into the same gymnasium, sat in the bleachers, and watched practice. His eyes were immediately drawn to a kid named Dennis Rodman, who displayed the natural ability and work ethic that rarely exists in the shadows of big-time basketball.

His heart raced, but from experience, he knew better than to buy into such illusions.

"I knew it was his first year in college, and I knew this kid was a Division One talent," Reisman said. "I knew I would never have a chance to recruit him. That's just the way it works."

Reisman took notes on two other players attending Cooke County, and on this evening, he came looking for confirmation, to see how they performed under game conditions.

But as Cooke County took the floor for warm-ups, something was wrong, something was missing.

Namely, Dennis Rodman.

"I asked somebody where he was at, and they told me he left school," Reisman said. "He hadn't completed an English class or something like that. He had flunked out of school."

Immediately, Reisman's bulldog instincts kicked in. Given the circumstances, this kid was no longer destined for the elite NCAA programs. This was just the kind of kid who needed what Reisman had to offer.

"That's the way small colleges operate," he said. "If a kid has grade problems, you try to get him focused. And if you can, you have a chance. I decided to hunt him down, but how do you find him? After all, Dallas is a city with two million people."

Undaunted, Reisman called the Registrar's Office at Cooke County the next day. He asked for Dennis Rodman's phone number, and no matter how hard he pleaded, he was turned down.

He waited a week, and called the same number. This time, a student employee picked up the phone.

"Ma'am, this is an emergency," Reisman said. "I need Dennis Rodman's phone number. I'm not asking for his transcript. Ma'am, this is an emergency, and I'm a friend of the family's. I have to find him. We're talking about this kid's life. This is a life-or-death situation. This is very important."

To Reisman, this was an emergency.

Just not the kind the young woman on the other end of the line was imagining at the moment.

"I don't think he wanted to come to Oklahoma at first, but his mother was a strong force, a driving force at the time."
Lonn Reisman, former assistant coach at Southeastern Oklahoma State

She relented, and Reisman had his number. He called Rodman's home, and Shirley answered. Reisman struck a cordial tone, telling Shirley that his school was very interested in recruiting Dennis. He said one of Dennis's boyhood friends—a kid named Emery Aaron—was also at Southeastern Oklahoma State. He had escaped the inherent troubles of Oak Cliff, found a new beginning in Durant, and was doing very well.

"I had to get her attention," Reisman said. "And anytime you know someone that the family knows, it helps break the ice."

In truth, Shirley needed no convincing. This was exactly what she had hoped for, and agreed for a meeting that following Saturday.

"The only problem was getting Dennis to cooperate," Shirley said.

As fate would have it, Dennis called home the next day. He had called his mother sporadically in the last few weeks, dropping hints that he was longing for home. This time, he sounded almost frantic. He was broke, he was lonely, he was going hungry out on his own.

Shirley relented, but with one stipulation: he had to be home on Saturday to meet with this basketball coach who had been calling the house. He had to recognize this opportunity and give it his full attention.

He agreed.

"He didn't apply himself when he got his first opportunity, and I knew that [attending] classes was very hard for Dennis," Shirley said. "But in my mind, this was his last chance."

In the meantime, Reisman did his homework. He discovered that Dennis's sisters were stars in high school and embarking on stellar collegiate careers. If they were so well grounded in discipline, what had gone wrong with their older brother?

"I'm thinking this must be a pretty mixed-up young man," Reisman said. "His mom was there, and I could tell that she cared. I knew he must've been in the shadows of his sisters."

"He needed a male to be around him, to lead him, to correct him."

Lonn Reisman

Armed with a steady sales pitch and the company of the head basketball coach, a man named Jack Hedden, Reisman pulled up to the curb on Sunnyvale Drive in Oak Cliff. They waited in the car for a few minutes, and at precisely 8:00 A.M. they left the vehicle and rang the doorbell.

Shirley Rodman was awake and ready for the moment.

Dennis was locked in his bedroom, asleep. He was rousted by his mother, but remained completely unresponsive. He was backing off on his promise, and informed his mother that he wasn't in the mood to talk with anybody.

After waiting a half-hour in Shirley's living room, Reisman and Hedden walked toward Rodman's bedroom. They began talking to a door, pleading with Rodman to come out, if only for a few minutes.

The door finally opened, and Rodman emerged in his underwear.

"Didn't matter to me, because I wasn't leaving," Reisman said. "If it took me until four P.M., he was going to come out of that door, and I was going to be there. When I saw him for the first time, we looked at each other, and he just mumbled something."

Reisman recognized this was not going to be easy. He dropped the extensive sales pitch, and made a simple offer:

"I told him to get in the car and come with me to Southeastern Oklahoma," Reisman said. "I told him we'd look around for a couple of hours, and then I'd bring him right back home. I don't think he wanted to go, but his mother was a very strong force. I kept prodding, 'C'mon, Dennis. C'mon, Dennis. What do you have to lose?'"

Before he knew it, Reisman, Hedden, and Rodman were in the car, heading to a school just ninety miles away from home. Just a few miles into the drive, Reisman brought up Emery Aaron, and Rodman immediately responded. A bond was beginning to form, and Reisman sensed as much.

On campus, Reisman and Rodman took a walk. Reisman talked about the intimate nature of the school, attended by just over five thousand students. He drove Rodman around town pointing out the convenience of a small community. They talked about life, about the pressures Dennis must have felt competing with such successful siblings. It was standard stuff, but Reisman noticed that Rodman's detached demeanor had done an about-face.

"We really got a good feeling about him," Reisman said. "He was showing us warmth, more warmth than you usually get from kids."

Their final destination was the basketball arena. They walked across the floor, and took a seat in the bleachers.

Reisman let it all hang out.

"Dennis, I saw you play one afternoon at Cooke County, I watched you during practice," Reisman said.

Rodman was silent.

Reisman continued.

"You know, I've never had a professional player play for me. But I think you have a chance to play professional basketball."

Rodman was stunned.

"No way!" he said.

"I really think you can," Reisman countered.

"Why?"

"You have something special, Dennis. You run the floor very well for your size. You play with a lot of heart and courage. You have what it takes. So, c'mon, I'm going to whip your butt in a game of H-O-R-S-E."

Reisman pulled a ball out of the office, and he and Rodman began to play. All the while, Reisman filled Rodman's ears with music he had never heard before, bountiful compliments about his natural ability and unlimited potential.

Like a brittle sponge, Rodman absorbed every word.

When they were done, Reisman told Rodman to get dressed, and when he returned, they met back on the gymnasium floor.

Reisman took a deep breath.

"Dennis, I'd really like you to sign with us. Take your time, think about it, but know that we really want you."

Rodman smiled.

"I'm signing today," Rodman said.

Reisman was stunned, as any recruiter would be. He had found his star, a rare talent who could make an immediate impact in his program. And just hours after the discovery, he had hit the mother lode.

"I was absolutely floored," Reisman said.

"The reason he went to Oklahoma is he had to get away from me. I had hounded him for nineteen years."
Shirley Rodman

They found Hedden, and they all convened in his office. They went over the decision again, to make sure there was no confusion. Hedden laid down the law, telling his new recruit that he would be working his tail off for the next three years, but the rewards could be enormous.

Rodman nodded, took the pen, and signed without a hint of apprehension.

Reisman drove Dennis back to Dallas late that afternoon, and while Shirley was concerned about her son attending school in a rural, lily-white farming community, she knew there was no other choice.

"There is nothing but the school and farmers in that perimeter," Shirley said. "But he needed to get away from me because I had been hounding him for nineteen years."

When Reisman returned to school, he made a few phone calls, and began talking to some of his friends in the business. Word had gotten out about this incredibly talented player who flunked out of

Cooke County, a kid who was sitting at home doing nothing, a kid who was there for the taking.

Reisman leaned back in his chair and laughed.

"A couple of big-name schools had just heard about Dennis, and they were ready to go after him," Reisman said. "But I got there first."

If you're a recruiter, this type of story comes around once in a lifetime. If you're lucky.

"It was mind-boggling," Reisman said. "You have all these talented kids playing at all those five-star basketball camps, and I find this kid in the ghettos of Dallas, cleaning cars, cleaning the airport. But I guess it got to the point where his mother said 'You have to do this or you're out of the house again.' "

five
WONDER WORM

"At the time, Dennis just took to my son. Why?

Nobody has ever known."

James Rich

n May of 1983, Dennis Rodman cleaned out his room, packed his clothes in a duffel bag, and boarded a Greyhound bus for Oklahoma.

Ever since signing a letter of intent with Southeastern Oklahoma State, Rodman had been consumed with his new opportunity. Unlike his time at Cooke County, he knew this was for real, and there was no turning back. He was suddenly armed with a vision, a tangible chance to correct all wrongs. He believed in the heavy praise of his new coaches, and realized this was a fast track to catch up with his siblings, to show up all of the people who had labeled him a lost cause.

In order to be eligible for the upcoming season, he needed to attend summer school. With a revamped attitude and a sense of direction guiding him for the first time in his life, this was not going to be a problem.

In fact, Rodman was actually diving into his new life with surprising vigor.

"I went to visit him in the dormitories early in the summer," Reisman said. "He opened the door, and I caught him pressing his pants, getting ready to go to class."

Reisman's visit was not without purpose. In order to keep his pockets lined with change over the summer, Reisman thought that Rodman should work as a counselor at Southeastern's annual basketball camp for youngsters. He told Rodman it would be easy work, easy money, and a chance to become immediately integrated into the community.

He told Rodman to come down to the gym after class, meet some of the kids, and take it from there.

And so began one of the strangest, most inexplicable episodes in the life of Dennis Rodman.

The five-day camp was no different from hundreds of others that take place all over the country, where gymnasiums burst with eager children of all skill levels, learning the fundamentals of basketball in a structured fashion.

Yet for Bryne Rich, a twelve-year-old from neighboring Bokchito, it was a turning point in a life saddled with trauma.

Only ten months earlier, Rich had gone quail hunting with a few friends, a hobby as natural and common in these parts as shooting basketballs in the driveway. They were barely inside the forest be-hind the Richs' expansive farm when they began testing their shot-guns.

Tragically, Bryne's shotgun went off as he was reloading, killing his best friend.

He was sickened with grief and haunted by guilt, unsure if he could ever face the world again. And although he was absolved by the family of his best friend and constantly soothed by his own parents, the pain was a constant companion.

Finally, after much coaxing, Bryne's parents convinced him to attend the basketball camp at Southeastern.

"I was just starting to get on my feet," Bryne said. "For the longest time, I was just down. Just down and out. I didn't want to be around anybody."

But the basketball camp was sort of a summer ritual for Bryne, the kind that connected the dots of a dream still in its infancy. And despite an accident that pierced his innocence, Bryne's dream of becoming a professional basketball player was still intact.

Bryne had not yet heard of Southeastern's prized recruit, but on the first day of camp, he listened to every word his coach had to say. Bryne concentrated only on running through the demons, find-ing solace in the heavy sweat and sneakers squeaking on the pol-ished floor. He was always a hard-nosed player, diving after loose balls, determined to outhustle everyone. Now, his intensity was even more furious, and Rodman immediately took to the young player.

"He was always pushing me," Bryne said. "I don't know why he favored me. Maybe because I was always smaller than the other guys, and I had to be aggressive. I think he liked my attitude; I think he liked the fight in me. But for some reason, he was always trying to help me."

Bryne became immediately attached to his new friend, and even though Rodman was ten years older and from a completely different world, the feeling was mutual. The catered attention continued each day in camp, and a ritual quickly developed: When camp was over, Bryne would call his mother and say he was staying late. While Rodman scrimmaged with his new teammates, Bryne would practice alone at a basket in the corner of the gym. When Rodman was finished, he would buy Bryne a soft drink, and they'd hang out for a little while.

Finally, sensing that the friendship would have the same shelf-life as the basketball camp, Bryne took a chance. He asked Rodman to join his family for dinner, and after the last day of camp, Rodman complied.

"Dennis really helped Bryne Rich out of a deep depression. There are not a lot of young men who would care enough to help out a young kid."

Lonn Reisman

James Rich knew he was bringing a guest home for dinner as he arrived at Southeastern that night.

He didn't know that his son's new friend was six feet eight.

Or twenty-two years of age.

Or black.

"He told us, 'I've got this friend coming home with me, a guy I met at basketball camp,' " James said. "Of course, he didn't say he was black. That didn't mean anything to us. I used to work with black people before. But maybe [Bryne] thought it might mean something."

Turns out, the only difficulty was getting their dinner guest to speak. Pat Rich was immediately struck by Dennis's shy nature, but his grin was infectious. And it was clear that there was a budding friendship between Dennis and Bryne, and that Bryne was quickly shedding his shell of despondency.

Dennis didn't go back to school that evening, instead sharing a room with Bryne. And so it went for the next three weeks.

Dennis would get up in the morning and accompany Pat to Southeastern. Dennis would attend summer school, and instead of returning to the dormitories, he would hitch a ride with Pat back to the farm in Bokchito.

James and Pat never questioned the arrangement, despite such rapid developments. In Bryne, they saw a child who was gobbling up all the life he had missed in the past ten months, a sudden reemergence of exuberance that was finally healing his soul. In Dennis, they saw a young man obviously deficient of the subtleties a strong family takes for granted.

James Rich could also see to the core of their new guest, and found much empathy. Like Rodman, he was a quiet man. Like Rodman, his father had left home when he was three, and he knew what the scars looked like.

"He had pretty low self-esteem; he didn't have the confidence or the ability to express himself," Pat said. "But rather than saying things, rather than giving advice, we just accepted him for what he was. We made him feel a part of our family.

"I don't want to take anything away from his mother, but he didn't have a father to give him attention. I didn't claim to be his biological mother, but I mothered him, and I mothered him like he was my own son. He met Bryne's needs at the time, but more than anything, we just really enjoyed Dennis being around."

Rodman developed an affinity for the earthly feel of a ranching family. He learned to fish at a pond in the backyard, bounced around gleefully in the seat of the Riches' tractor, and blended in with Bryne's circle of friends.

"Back then, Dennis was nothing," Bryne said. "No one knew who he was, or whether he'd be a good college basketball player. It was like meeting a stranger who just fit right in.

"I know it seems really weird, him being nine to ten years older than me. But he was just like a kid at heart. And he had taken so much off my mind, helping me so much without even knowing. We'd go eat together, play video games together, play basketball together. Whatever we did, we did it together."

"He just showed up one day, and almost immediately became part of our family."
Pat Rich, whose family sheltered Rodman

As the summer wafted by, Rodman's immaturity began to surface. One afternoon, James and Pat were snagging catfish at the pond in their backyard when the serenity was polluted by a string of obscenities. They looked up toward the house, and there was Rodman, shooting baskets by himself and swearing at the top of his lungs.

"He was letting out all these big, ugly words," Pat said. "We were just standing there and looking. Finally, my husband hollered all the way from the pond, 'Hey, cut that out!' But I think he was expressing some anger, I think he was releasing something, just venting."

He was, in fact, screaming for attention and discipline, to be included in the family guidelines. He had spent most of his life in the lazy zone of an outsider, where freedom was abundant, but direction absent. He had spent nearly two decades testing the patience and anger of his mother. Now it was paternal guidance that Rodman was craving.

"This was all a very good experience for him," Pat said. "He had always lived in the city, and now he was isolated out on a farm. It's just a whole different life out here. You don't have any neighbors close by, you don't have any streets. You have fields and machinery and cows. He experienced our life, the experience of catching a fish for the first time, and all of that made him grow.

"But I had three boys of my own, and with all this chaos going on, Dennis would sit back and laugh at me when he saw me the most serious. One day, I was trying to make them all mind, and I ran into the patio door, thinking it was open. It knocked me down on my back, and Dennis just laughed. But my husband would get on his case big-time, he would get on him like a stepchild. There were times when he hurt Dennis's feelings, and Dennis would cry like a baby. But I think, deep down, he liked that. I think that's exactly what he needed."

As the fall semester at Southeastern beckoned, Rodman finally headed back to campus. He showed tremendous aptitude, and remarkable endurance. He swallowed every ounce of criticism from Hedden and Reisman, accepting the challenges they laid on their new star from the start of fall practices.

"One of the most coachable players I've ever been around," Reisman said. "He never saw himself as the star; he saw himself as a team member."

The Savages were scheduled to open their season on the road against Langston University, and a new era in Southeastern basketball was about to begin. Before they boarded the bus for the three-hour trip, Rodman approached Reisman.

"Coach, I hope I don't disappoint you tonight," Rodman said.

"You won't," Reisman said.

And he didn't. In his first game of organized basketball. Rodman scored 24 points, making 9 of 16 shots. He made 6 of 10 free throws. And he grabbed 19 rebounds.

Southeastern defeated Langston 56–55, but not without a moment of revelation.

Late in the game, with Southeastern clinging to a tenuous lead, Hedden instructed his team to go into a four-corner stall. The element of unpredictability was how Rodman would react under duress, in the waning moments of a close game. To play it safe, Rodman was instructed to stand in one corner of the court, and when the ball came his way, he was to get it back to a teammate as soon as possible.

The ball did come his way, but Rodman's defender overreacted. There was an open path to the basket, and Rodman seized the moment.

"He caught the ball, took off, and dunked it," Reisman said. "And right then, I thought to myself, 'This kid is special.' We didn't even know he could handle the ball, but we underestimated his instincts for the game."

In his second game against Austin College in Sherman, Texas, Rodman was even better. He scored 40 points on 18-of-24 shooting, hauled down 13 rebounds, and the Savages breezed to an 81–67 victory.

Hedden and Reisman knew they had a star in the making, and the community was starting to buzz about the basketball team at Southeastern. While the coaching staff began to feel a bit uneasy with Rodman's dependence on the Riches, how he insisted that Bryne travel on the team bus after games, how he would forgo the dorms and stay at the farm in Bokchito, they acquiesced to Rodman's wishes.

They sensed that, somehow, his ties with the Rich family were beneficial to Rodman. And midway through the season, they anointed Bryne as the team water boy, and he would sit on the end of the bench during games.

37

"Bryne had been at our camps in the past, and Dennis really helped Bryne out of a depression that had taken over his life," Reisman said. "I really thought a lot about Dennis helping that youngster come out of being withdrawn.

"And it served Dennis, too. He found somebody who looked up to him. When he was growing up, everyone looked up to his sisters, to Debra and Kim. Now somebody was saying, 'Dennis, you're special to me.' And maybe that was the first time that ever happened to Dennis.

"I think Dennis's confidence grew from that summer on the farm. He didn't have a lot of confidence when we first saw him, but you could see him start to mature as a young man.

"I had known Pat and James for a long time, and I think they gave Dennis some stability. He had a place to stay, and if he wanted to go and work on the farm, that was fine. All of our players had different relationships with different people all over the place. As long as it didn't affect his performance, we decided it wouldn't be a problem."

To the contrary. Rodman's commitment to basketball only flourished. There would be nights when Reisman walked into the locker room at halftime and found Rodman crying.

"I'd ask him what was wrong, and he would mumble that he wasn't playing very well," Reisman said. "I'd look at the stat sheet and see he had fifteen points and fifteen rebounds. You could tell he was raw and inexperienced, but he had incredible enthusiasm. The kid just loved to play."

"Even back then, he just wanted to play, and he just wanted to rebound. He didn't care if he scored a point or not. That's pretty rare with kids these days."

Harold Harmon, sports information director
at Southeastern Oklahoma State

The Savages finished the season with an 18-9 record, and Rodman was remarkable. He averaged 26.1 points and 12.6 rebounds a game in his inaugural season, and Southeastern was back on the sporting map for the first time in decades.

Southeastern had come close to winning an NAIA national championship in 1956, led by a three-time All-American named Jim Spivey.

Suddenly, they had burst out of a thirty-year shroud of anonymity behind another sensation. Rodman came to school with a strange nickname—"Worm"—which was born from the way he would wiggle while playing pinball as a youngster. In Durant, that moniker was enhanced, and now Rodman was known as "Wonder Worm."

The excitement was palpable, and not just because of the glitzy record. Rodman had become quite the entertainer on the basketball court, pumping his fists and pointing to the crowd every time he scored.

To opponents, he was a source of agitation, a hot dog. To his school, he was a rare celebrity who awakened a dormant program.

"Dennis was a little bitty boy who was in the limelight for the first time," said Harold Harmon, who still serves as Southeastern's sports information director and sports editor of the *Durant Daily Democrat*. "People were calling him a hot dog, but that wasn't the case. Dennis was doing that stuff on Tuesday afternoon in practice, diving on the floor, diving into the bleachers, crashing through people. Even in practice, when a teammate made a good play, he was excited."

And it was downright contagious. The Savages roared into the postseason, thumping Northeastern Oklahoma State 86–68 in the first round of the District Nine playoffs.

Their next game was against Southwestern Oklahoma State, which had earned the top seed in the tournament.

Near the end of the first half, Rodman snared a rebound, fired an outlet pass to Phillip Stephens, the team's point guard, and began racing downcourt.

Stephens took three dribbles, crossed halfcourt, and launched the ball toward the basket.

"I'm thinking, 'What is this kid doing?' " Reisman said. "Out of nowhere, here comes a deer . . . that's what [Rodman] ran like, a Ferrari. He catches the ball over the rim, and dunks the ball behind his back.

"He received a standing ovation from everyone in the gym, *their* gym. The whole crowd of three thousand just stood up, appreciating what he did."

It was the crowning moment of the season for Rodman, who had 42 points and 24 rebounds in the Savages' stunning 81–64 victory.

The Savages would be eliminated in their next game, but finished with a 20-10 record. And the kid from nowhere had soared to national prominence, completing a stunning season with an array of accolades.

Postseason included, he shot an amazing 62 percent from the field. He was named a first-team NAIA All-American. He was selected as both the District Nine Player of the Year and the Oklahoma Intercollegiate Conference Player of the Year.

And it was only the beginning.

"It's like Dennis opened his eyes, and saw a different world," Reisman said. "He sensed a measure of self-worth, that 'I am becoming something. I am making something out of my life. I see a different direction, and it's positive.' That just lit him up."

six
SPEED BUMPS

"**From Day One, I knew there was going to be trouble. I knew he was going to encounter some bad people. They use the *N* word over there.**"
Shirley Rodman

Buoyed by his accomplishments, Rodman again spent the following summer in Bokchito. In the course of one basketball season, his identity went from janitor to celebrity, and for the most part, he was the toast of Southeastern Oklahoma State.

He had become instantly popular with the student body, and naturally, with the young women as well.

"One day, he comes over to our house, and he's sick as a dog," Reisman said. "He comes in, my wife puts him on the couch, gives him some aspirin, and starts babying him. He was there a couple of hours when my wife looks out the window and sees a girl sitting in the car."

"Dennis, who is that in the car?" she asked.

"Oh, that's just a girl I'm with today," Rodman replied.

"But Dennis, don't you think you should ask her in?" she countered.

"No, I'm feeling a little better now," he said.

And just like that, Rodman bounced off the couch, rejoining his incredibly patient friend.

But with his burgeoning popularity came the flip side of his environment—the dark whispers of racism. It was one thing for a black athlete to show up at the college and dominate on the basketball court. Such acceptance, however, didn't translate as easily when it came to interracial dating in rural Oklahoma.

The racial tension had surfaced the previous summer. He had seen the discomfort in Pat Rich, who had felt the peer pressure of housing a black boy in a white community. She readily admits that she would sometimes take the scenic route to the university to avoid being seen in the same automobile as Dennis, thereby avoiding the loose talk and neighborhood gossip.

And he was warned by his mother, who was not at all comfortable with Dennis's new life. She experienced twinges of maternal jealously after learning that Dennis had become so comfortable and so welcome at the Rich residence. But she was also fearful that her son would be subject to overt racism, and she knew how easily his feelings were hurt.

"I see him now, yapping and carrying on. Back then, he didn't have the confidence or the ability to express himself."

Pat Rich

At first, the racial implications were nothing Rodman hadn't felt before. He seemed impenetrable, almost amused at the predicament he had caused Pat.

But now that Rodman was an overnight success, evil and petty jealousy were seeping through the cracks, turning the tone of racial slurs from ignorant to malicious.

It was starting to get to Rodman.

"We went through some real prejudiced slurs," Pat said. "I suffered tremendously. Dennis would always come home crying, and so would I. I got a lot of flak from that."

Although it didn't show on the court, a sense of bitterness began to overtake Rodman. He opened his junior season with another string of dominating performances, leading the Savages to a 4-0 record.

But he began showing familiar signs of self-destruction, showing up late for practice, blowing off a few classes. Hedden and Reisman responded by pushing Rodman even harder.

"He needed a male to correct him, to lead him in the right direction," Reisman said. "When he did something wrong, I wouldn't let him get out of it. If he missed a class, I went and found him. We had to jump on the little things, and we had to establish that early in his career. Because if I let that go, they would turn into big things.

"He was under a microscope in a community that size, and whatever he did was going to be magnified."

Hedden and Reisman sensed that Rodman needed to get back on campus, to blend in with the students and his fellow athletes. They demanded that he move out of the Riches' house and back into the dormitories. It was a move that Rodman's mother vigorously supported.

But Rodman was appalled, incensed at the blanket of authority that had been thrown over him. Initially, he complied, but not without a certain indignance.

And one day, after practice, Rodman quit the team.

"He really didn't care for his surroundings," Bryne said. "It was a small school, a small town. He was used to the big city. A few times he wanted to quit, to go back with his old friends, and it took him a while to get used to it. I don't think he'd ever have stayed if we didn't come into his life."

The issue of racism was a logical source for Rodman's sudden display of surliness. But how real was it, and how much was just Rodman reverting to bad habits?

"I'm not going to say there weren't a few bad times," Reisman said. "I wasn't with him every second of every day. But the people he was around thought a lot of him, and backed him one hundred percent. No matter where you go—Dallas, Chicago, Durant—there will be things that hurt your feelings.

"I'm not going to say Dennis didn't get his feelings hurt because Dennis takes things to heart. It bothers him when people say things. But in all the years he played for me, all the butt-chewings he took, all the times that I was on him constantly, he never said one word back to me."

Said Harold Harmon: "This is southern Oklahoma. There are rednecks here. They're everywhere. But I don't recall Dennis having that bad a time with it. On the court, we heard him take more than anyone had to take, and all he would do was grin and dunk. There were whites and blacks saying things, but they were only trying to get to Rodman, the basketball player."

Whether the enemy was real or perceived, Rodman was once again rebelling. He left the dorms and went back to Bokchito. He was standing firm in his decision, telling Bryne and Pat that he had endured enough.

And then James Rich came home, heard about the developments, and told Dennis to get in the truck.

They went for a long ride, and somewhere in the middle, James began to speak.

"Dennis what are you doing?"

"I quit. I'm going back to Dallas."

"Dennis, why do you want to go back home? You'll never amount to anything up there. You've got a chance to play ball. You've got a chance to do something special. You're wasting the best part of your life."

Silence.

Rodman was listening, learning, obeying.

"He was pissed off at his coach," James said. "I didn't know what he was going to do, but I thought he had a future. I wanted him to stay in school, and he listened to me. I guess he kind of always looked up to me because he was looking for a father. And I stood up to him."

Rodman instantly complied, and returned to the team as if nothing had happened. The Savages continued their domination, finishing the regular season with a 20-7 record.

"When he got pissed off and quit the basketball team, I told him, "Dennis, you're wasting the best part of your life." I guess he just listened."

James Rich

In the first game of the District Nine playoffs, Rodman scored a career-high 51 points with 19 rebounds against Bethany Nazarene College. The Savages again reached the finals of the tournament, and were one victory away from a trip to the National Tournament in Kansas City.

On the eve of their biggest game in years, Reisman received a call from Billy Conaway, the team manager who roomed with Rodman during the postseason.

"It's eleven o'clock at night, and Billy tells me that Dennis is terribly sick, that I wouldn't believe how sick he was," Reisman said. "I run up there, take his temperature, and it's 104.5."

They rushed Rodman to the emergency room in Durant, where he was diagnosed with a severe case of tonsilitis. He was given a megadose of antibiotics, and finally released at 4:00 A.M.

"We put him to bed, and we told the doctors we would monitor him, see if the fever breaks," Reisman said. "So every two hours, we made him drink a quart of Gatorade and swallow two aspirin. He's lying in bed moaning, and I'm playing doctor."

By three o'clock in the afternoon, Rodman's temperature had dipped to 100.

The coaching staff made a decision.

Rodman would play only if his temperature was normal by tip-off. If nothing else, maybe he could make it to the game, and inspire his teammates just by showing up.

They got to the arena, and Reisman instructed Conaway to slice up twelve oranges and put them on ice, just in case Rodman played. During breaks in the action, he reasoned, Rodman could suck on the oranges for strength.

Reisman turned to Rodman in the locker room.

"Dennis, how do you feel?"

"Coach, I'm playing."

"Okay, but not if you're running a fever."

Two minutes before tip-off, Reisman stuck a thermometer in Rodman's mouth.

It read 98.6.

"And I know why," Reisman said. "It was all that aspirin he had in him."

Regardless, Rodman got dressed and took the floor. He scored 24 points with 10 rebounds and the Savages edged East Central University, 74–68.

They were going to the National Tournament.

But first, Rodman was going back to the hospital.

"How many kids would've done that?" Reisman said. "He wanted that championship."

It wouldn't come. Two games later, Rodman was held to nine points and five rebounds, and the Savages were eliminated by the College of Charleston, 60–43. It was just the second time in his career that he had not scored in double figures, and the second straight season that ended with a crushing loss.

But aside from duplicating the same array of postseason awards, Rodman had set foot in a new arena.

With a 40-point, 17-rebound performance in the opening game of the National Tournament, Rodman's name had been scribbled on the notepads of professional scouts in attendance. He was a name to watch, and the evaluation slips were being sent to general managers across the NBA.

He had entered the loop.

"It was just what we had told him from the day he got here," Reisman said. "And now he was hearing it from other people as well."

Yet as Rodman's head swelled with his growing notoriety, he began taking liberties with the Riches' belongings—like borrowing the car without warning, or strutting around school with a few pieces of Pat's jewelry.

And then it got real bad.

"We were out of town and he had written some hot checks on us," Pat said. "We were mad at him. We had to withdraw ourselves from him for a while. It was time for discipline, a time-out."

"I'd get on him like I'd get on my own kids. But I never would do it in front of everybody else. I'd take him for a ride in my truck, and we'd talk. I didn't want him to think we were getting on him because he was black."

James Rich

After it was discovered that Dennis had used the Riches' checking account without permission, he was kicked off the farm, just as he was booted out of his mother's home a few year earlier.

He moved back into the dormitories, again penalized for his mercurial talent of pushing the envelope too far. He was separated from the Riches for two weeks, but in a familiar twist in the Rodman saga, it was Pat who was burdened with guilt.

"I could see that Bryne wasn't smiling much anymore, and things weren't very chipper around here without Dennis," Pat said. "He brought a lot of joy and laughter in our lives, him just being black and different than the rest of us. Bryne, he moped around. He knew Dennis did wrong, but I could tell he missed him.

"Just for the love of Bryne, I decided everyone deserves a second chance. I would always see him on campus because I was going to school at the same time. And one day, he was standing alone, out in the rain. I was in a hurry to get to my car, but he just looked lonely and lost . . . I don't know what it was, but it was almost as if a magnet drew me in that direction."

It was, in fact, one of the perplexing powers of Dennis Rodman, a strange gift that he has carried with him his entire life. For he is as endearing as he is infuriating, and no matter how hard you try, it's impossible to dislike him, impossible not to extend second chances, and third chances, and fourth chances . . .

"I said, 'Dennis, everybody deserves a second chance. If you'd like to come back with me and have dinner with us, you're welcome. Bryne misses you.' " Pat said. "I could tell that made him happy."

Rodman's final season at Southeastern was the pinnacle of a grand experiment. He had developed a passion for weightlifting, and gained nearly twenty pounds of sinewy muscle. He put the Savages on his shoulders, and they rode to new heights.

He grabbed a career-high 32 rebounds in one victory, and led the Savages to a 22-game winning streak that ended in a loss to Arkansas-Monticello in the National Tournament semifinals.

The national championship had once again eluded Rodman and Southeastern, but with a consolation victory over St. Thomas Aquinas (New York), they would finish third in the nation. Rodman ended his career with a dazzling explosion, scoring 46 points in the victory over Aquinas, and his 32 rebounds tied the all-time single-game rebounding record.

The Savages finished 30-4 in Rodman's final season, and during his three-year stay at Southeastern, they posted a lofty 74-22 record.

Rodman became a three-time first-team NAIA All-American, averaging 25.7 points and 15.7 rebounds over his career. And as a senior, his rebounding average of 17.8 led the NAIA.

Was he playing against the best players in the nation?

Of course not.

But who's to say where Rodman would've landed had he jumped on board with an established powerhouse?

Just like his relationship with the Riches, his ties with Southeastern Oklahoma State were mutually beneficial, a strange meshing of identities that worked out perfectly.

"I think, overall, Southeastern was very good for him," Reisman said. "He came at a time when we needed him, and he needed us. It was a special thing.

"It was the only place he could've come at the time where the situation was demanding enough, where the system matched his skills, and where there was room for him to succeed.

"If he went somewhere bigger, he would've been hidden. He was shy, introverted, he needed a pat on the behind. If he would've got caught up at a big school, I don't know if he would've survived."

seven
PARTING WAYS

"Dennis has been fortunate, and he needs to know this. It's like he's had this guardian angel sitting on his shoulder from the moment he started playing basketball."
Lonn Reisman

 ennis Rodman boarded a plane for Hawaii, venturing into a foreign land with a dream he could barely comprehend.

He had been invited to participate in the Aloha Classic, the first in a series of predraft camps for NBA prospects. His college résumé was sparkling, and yet to Rodman, it had happened so fast that it all seemed surreal. In the space of three years, his identity had changed dramatically, and yet his perspective was light years behind. His self-esteem was lagging behind his talent, and all this talk of professional basketball made his head spin.

With a binding commitment to outhustling his opponent, he found that he could dominate small-college basketball. But it wasn't Division I, and Rodman knew it. And with that knowledge came considerable doubt.

He was assigned a hotel room with John Salley, one of the stars from a loaded Georgia Tech squad.

"He was shocked by even the fact that he was in Hawaii, playing against what was considered the best players in the country," Salley said. "He was so excited he almost cried."

Rodman turned in a solid performance over the next few days, becoming the camp's leading rebounder.

Then he said good-bye to his roommate, and boarded another plane.

"The last thing I said to him was, "I'll see you in the pros,' " Salley said. "He was like, 'Yeah right.' "

The next stop was the Portsmouth Invitational, a prestigious camp held in Virginia. Rodman's confidence was growing and he was superb, earning the camp's MVP award.

By now, it was becoming clear that Rodman had NBA talent. The Milwaukee Bucks, in particular, were highly interested in Rodman, and had dispatched a scout to watch him play in Durant two or three times over the past few months.

The last stop was a camp in Chicago, and strangely, Rodman bombed out. He played nowhere near his capabilities, had trouble getting up and down the court, and appeared drained.

There was a reason.

The Detroit Piston's hierarchy huddled in a Chicago hotel room during the camp to discuss their options. They were interested in Rodman, but curious why he had gotten chewed up in the opening day of camp.

They called in one of the trainers who was working with them at the camp to ask about Rodman and got a straight explanation. "The kid has a serious asthma problem; I'm not sure if anyone else knows about it."

One member of the hierarchy suggested maybe it was better that Rodman's problem remain undiagnosed. Whether the trainer followed, understood, or even heard the suggestion is unclear, but Rodman's performance did not improve.

As one observer noted "Teams dropped off him like flies."

The Pistons knew they could steal Rodman in the second round, especially after the final impression he had left in Chicago.

"Dennis needed our family, and we needed him. It was like peaches and cream."

Pat Rich

On draft day, 1986, Rodman had returned to Bokchito for what he and the Riches hoped would be a massive celebration. While Pat prepared Rodman's favorite dinner, the man of the hour sprawled out on the Riches' living room floor, glued to the television.

Salley, his new friend from Hawaii, was selected by the Pistons in the first round. And there was the complement of big names taken early: Maryland's Len Bias was chosen by the Boston Celtics; with a pair of selections, the Cleveland Cavaliers nabbed both North Carolina's Brad Daugherty and Miami of Ohio's Ron Harper; the New York Knicks opted for Kentucky's Kenny "Sky" Walker; and the Dallas Mavericks chose Michigan's Roy Tarpley.

But there were some strange choices as well. The Bulls used their first-round pick on Brad Sellers, a toothpick from Ohio State. The Denver Nuggets had two picks, and opted for St. Joseph's Maurice

Martin and Duke's Mark Alarie. And the Los Angeles Lakers opted for Notre Dame's Ken Barlow.

The first round expired without a taker, and Rodman remained motionless on the floor.

"We all just sat there," James Rich said. "You know, Dennis really didn't believe he was going to get drafted."

But the Pistons picked third in the second round, and knew precisely what they were doing. And with the twenty-seventh selection overall, Detroit took a chance on the unknown, untapped kid from Southeastern Oklahoma.

"When they called his name, it was not reality to Dennis," Pat Rich said. "He just couldn't believe what was happening to him."

And then the phone rang.

It was the Pistons, requesting Rodman's presence for a news conference.

DENNIS RODMAN'S COLLEGIATE CAREER

YEAR	GAMES	POINTS	REBOUNDS	FIELD GOAL PERCENTAGE
1983/84	30	26.0	13.1	.618
1984/85	32	26.8	15.9	.648
1985/86	34	24.4	17.8	.645
TOTAL	96	25.7	15.7	.637

Just like that, it was time to find a new family.

"It was a happy day," Pat Rich said. "But in ways, it was kind of sad. We knew he was heading off into a new life.

"It was just all so unreal. If anyone would've told me when I was a junior in high school that I'd be a surrogate mother for a black boy, I'd say you're out of your mind.

"It's not just the idea of [being] black, it's being associated with someone who went from being a regular person to a celebrity. It was a great growing process for all of us. I'm more open-minded now, and I try to help other people overcome their prejudices. I'm a counselor, and I can relate to black boys because I helped Dennis through a lot of his struggles.

"I do one-on-one counseling, and I've had people come into my office after a year or so and say, 'Why didn't you tell me you're the one who raised Dennis Rodman? You are the person who did this?' It's opened a lot of doors."

Indeed, Pat, who earned her master's degree in psychology from Southeastern Oklahoma State, now works as a counselor at a mental health facility. Her identity has been strengthened, her perspective broadened.

James still tends to the farm, but is also treasurer of Rich Erosion, a landscaping company that employs two of his three sons.

And then there's Rodman Excavation, a construction company in Texas run by the Riches' middle son, Barry, which employs over two hundred people in the Dallas area.

"We now have two companies because of Dennis," Pat Rich said. "We have people from this town working for us, putting bread and butter on the tables in this town."

But more than any monetary windfall, there is a legacy that will lock the Riches into the history books, assuring some form of immortality.

They were once a family perfectly content with the anonymity of rural America, anchored to the deep roots of a six hundred-acre farm. And then, out of nowhere, a strange tornado touched down and changed everything.

It is the kind of unexpected twist that forever changes the family crest. And now, after you've fostered a giant celebrity, how do you go back to planting peanuts? How do you fill the void of an exhilarating rush, one that lands smack in the middle of a structured existence and disrupts everything . . . for the better?

After all, life had been a quiet hum for decades, driven by the slow pulse indigenous to a ranching community in the middle of nowhere. And then a kid named Dennis Rodman shows up at your door, and immediately, there is chaos.

There were stereotypes to overcome, unexamined prejudices that needed liberation. There was a strange sense of shame at first, painful sensitivity to the whispers of townfolk who wondered what in the hell was going on with Pat and James Rich.

Then there was empowerment, a palpable bonding of cultures that prevailed in the face of lingering racism, a family that not only grew to love this black, inner-city misfit, but to depend on his quirks more than they ever anticipated.

But most of all, there was a vibrancy, a flat-out goofiness that has never been replaced.

"This wasn't a story that unfolded in front of my eyes," Pat Rich said. "This was a story that hit me upside the head. To be honest, I still can't believe it happened."

Whatever the reason, Dennis Rodman became an unofficial member of the Rich family for three years. And even if you tried, you couldn't conceive of a more improbable pairing.

"We clothed him, fed him, gave him money and met his needs," Pat Rich said. "And he has certainly been a reward to our family. But I think we've been a reward to him, too. He went pro by staying here. What more could you ask for, to fall in love with our family and be loved and nurtured and supported? We laughed together, we cried together, we treated him as our own son."

Which bothered Shirley Rodman to no end.

Back at home in Dallas, she also watched the NBA draft, and carried on like she had won the lottery. Her baby had done the impossible, parlaying his first real commitment into the opportunity of a lifetime, a potential spot on an NBA roster.

But she was also relieved that his time with the Riches had come to an end. There was a certain maternal jealousy she had harbored during the past three years, a sense of emptiness and confusion about how her son could find solace in another home.

She felt robbed of attention, and to this day, the relationship between Shirley Rodman and the Rich family in Bokchito is undeniably strained.

"They hound him incessantly, and for some reason he feels so obligated to them," Shirley said. "That period in his life served a purpose, a time in which God ordained them to have Dennis, but that time is over.

"They're not the best people in the world. They have made a lot of money off of Dennis, and they have not been kind to me. They were on all of the talk shows talking about Dennis, and I got shut out in the process. He was a confused young man when he went [to Oklahoma], and the Riches just took over. It's one of the sore points in my life."

Pat Rich knows about the acrimony. She was listed as a coauthor on a book entitled *Rebound: The Dennis Rodman Story*, a book that details Rodman's entire stay with the Riches. She admits that her family has benefited from Rodman's success, but isn't about to apologize.

"We didn't let other people change our values, and that's why we were rewarded," Pat said. We gave our love, our time, and our home to Dennis because we wanted to. It was a reward that God gave us because he saw the struggles and hardship we went through, the persecution and ridicule we took, the fiery furnaces we went through raising Dennis.

"I don't claim to be his mother; it makes Mrs. Rodman mad. It gets under her skin. When we talk about helping Dennis, she says that Dennis worked for everything he got. That's true, but he had lots and lots of needs, and we helped fill those needs.

"She wants to forget that we ever existed. That's what really makes me angry. Never once did she say, "Thank y'all.' She's never showed us any gratitude."

In truth, such jealousy is a normal condition surrounding the phenomenon known as Dennis Rodman, no different from a pair of girlfriends who are fighting for his time. Neither gets her share, and they end up sniping at each other.

So now there are times when Pat will look out the window, glance at the basketball hoop in the driveway, and remember how Dennis once spent hours just dribbling and cussing, dribbling and cussing. There are times when she and her husband will sit in the living room, shaking their heads in wonder at the course of history, one that stopped and paused under their roof before gathering steam. And there are times when both Pat and James ache to see Dennis walk through the front door just one more time.

"It's amazing that Dennis Rodman was once in this house, lying on this floor, watching this television," Pat said. "Why didn't I know all of this back then? I would've washed his feet.

"Not long ago, we came home and there was a bouquet of fresh flowers sitting on our doorstep. They were from Dennis. But what we'd really like is for him to come back, to walk through that door, just like he used to.

"He calls it 'trippin'.' We'd love to just trip out, talk, and laugh all over again. I don't think he realizes how much we miss him."

eight

"I saw this marvelous athlete with an incredible gait. He was like a mustang out on a range, the kind of horse you don't even try to put a saddle on."
Chuck Daly

The draft had ended, and word was spreading among the Pistons that they may have pulled off a coup in the second round. The players knew all about Salley, a six-eleven center who had become Georgia Tech's all-time leader in blocked shots. But Dennis Rodman was a mystery.

One afternoon, Will Robinson, the Pistons' chief scout, walked into the team offices and spotted Isiah Thomas and Bill Laimbeer. He began raving over their find.

"Wait until you see this guy," Robinson said. "He'll get a rebound, throw the ball to halfcourt, and dunk on the other end."

Laimbeer and Thomas both rolled their eyes.

"Will, you're seventy-five years old, you're losing your mind," Laimbeer said.

"I'm serious," Robinson insisted. "Just wait and see. The guy goes nonstop all game long."

But when Rodman showed up at the Pistons' rookie camp in Windsor, Ontario, in 1986, he was out of his element. The drills were confusing, and the game moved incredibly fast.

He was no doubt in awe of his surroundings, and he froze under the pressure. Neither he nor Salley was adapting well, and they endured rookie hazing and the wrath of their coach, Chuck Daly.

"They failed miserably," Daly said. "They just weren't factors at all in any of the rookie games we monitored. They thought they would step right in and be stars and starters. But they looked awful.

"Everyone was saying we made a terrible mistake in drafting those two guys. It was actually a good thing for us. They signed [contracts] right away, and they went to work. They learned valuable lessons right off the bat. They suddenly realized what the next step was. It turned out to be a very positive thing for the team because I could work them in slowly, bring them off the bench. We became so defensive-oriented late in the game, and they were both tremendous assets."

Rodman started the 1986–87 season on the bench, backing up small forward Adrian Dantley, who was acquired in the off-season to provide the Pistons with inside scoring. But he was a quick study, and made the most of his minutes.

"Any time you have a guy out there who is productive and doesn't need the ball, it's a positive thing."

Doug Collins, NBA coach

He was tireless on the court, and a jumping jack under the basket. He worked his playing time up to fifteen minutes a game, an integral part of the Pistons' greatest asset—a dominating bench.

Playing with Laimbeer, Rick Mahorn, and Salley, he specialized in shutting down small forwards late in the game, and doing most of his rebounding on the offensive end. He averaged more points (6.5) than rebounds (4.3) as a rookie, but began stealing minutes from Dantley late in the game, a time when the Pistons put the clamp on their opponents.

"He was just trying to survive in the league," said Brendan Malone, who also served as one Daly's assistants. "If you look on tape, his body back then was much different than it is now. He was very lean, very wiry. He was just a role player on that team, but a very valuable role player."

Rodman also exuded the same childish enthusiasm that marked his career at Southeastern Oklahoma. He pumped his fists after every basket, instantly becoming a fan favorite in Detroit and an object of wrath everywhere else.

"He was a prolific rebounder in college. Granted, it was a small college in the middle of Podunk, USA."

Bill Laimbeer, former Detroit Piston

The Pistons finished the season 52-30, second behind Atlanta in the Central Division. But they were jelling near the playoffs, sweeping the Washington Bullets in the first round, and upsetting the

Hawks in the conference semifinals, winning a decisive Game 5 in Atlanta.

Up next were the Boston Celtics, a team that had won 59 games in the regular season, second only to the 65-17 Los Angeles Lakers, who were clearly the class of the league.

The Celtics won the first two games at the Boston Garden, but the Pistons rallied at home, thrashing the Celtics in Games 3 and 4. The series was tied, and the Pistons' confidence was growing.

The Pistons gave the Celtics all they could handle in Game 5, and for the hosts, the frustration was beginning to surface. After tangling with Laimbeer for a rebound, Celtics center Robert Parish went bonkers. He flailed his fists at Laimbeer, striking the Pistons' center three times before he fell to the floor.

The Pistons were on the verge of a colossal breakthrough, and they knew it.

They led 107–106 late, and the Celtics' last chance had seemingly ended when Rodman blocked a driving shot by Larry Bird. The Pistons had the ball with just five seconds left.

All they had to do was successfully inbound the ball.

They could not.

Unaware of Daly's pleas for a time-out, Isiah Thomas threw a soft, tentative pass to Laimbeer near the baseline. Bird read the play perfectly, intercepted the pass, and adroitly fed Dennis Johnson for a layup.

The Celtics prevailed, 108–107.

Parish was suspended for Game 6, making Bird's heroics even larger in magnitude. The Pistons forced a Game 7 at Boston Garden, but they were doomed, beaten by ghosts and leprechauns and Bird, whose iron will dictated the outcome.

Bird had scored 36 points in Game 5, 35 in Game 6, and 35 in the Celtics' decisive 117–114 victory.

The Celtics had outlasted the upstart Pistons in a violently physical series. And when the final buzzer sounded, Celtics guard Danny Ainge gloated in triumph, lingering on the court and imitating Rodman's celebratory dance.

"I'd been waiting to do that Dennis Rodman dance since the series began," Ainge said. "That wasn't intended for Detroit or anyone else on their team. Just Dennis Rodman."

The Pistons, numbed and embittered by a series that slipped through their fingers, were losers. And in the locker room afterward, they acted the part.

Rodman stood at his locker, seething in defeat. He had been jeered. He had been mocked. And he had been vanquished.

He was asked about the Celtics, and embarked on one of the most notorious postgame interviews in playoff history, sparking a controversy that crossed racial lines.

"The Finals won't last long," Rodman snapped. "I'll never root for Boston for as long as I live. They're not my favorite team, you know."

He was asked about Bird.

"He's not the greatest player in the NBA," Rodman said.

Okay, who is?

"Magic Johnson," Rodman said. "Nobody gives Magic credit. He got screwed out of the MVP last year."

He was informed that Bird had won three MVPs.

"He's white," Rodman said. "That's the only reason he gets it."

At a locker stall nearby in the cramped visitors' quarters of the Garden, Rodman's message was related to Thomas.

"I think Larry is a very, very good player," Thomas added. "He's an exceptional talent. But I'd have to agree with Rodman. If he were black, he'd be just another good guy."

The media knew it was in the midst of a major story. In the winners' locker room, they tracked down Bird, and told the Celtics superstar of Rodman's assessment.

"I'm very happy I'm white," Bird said.

He was asked about Rodman.

"He's a rookie," Bird said. "He'll learn."

Bird was then informed that Thomas had backed Rodman's verbal jab.

He sighed.

"It's a free world," Bird said. "We're not in Russia. You can say what you want to say. You don't have to like it."

Across the room, Celtics forward Kevin McHale wasn't as diplomatic.

"Someone ought to hang Dennis Rodman from the Silverdome ceiling and slap the shit out of him," he said.

Rodman had created a firestorm with his denunciation of Bird, and the Pistons were now taking the heat. Rodman's comments were attributed to the careless mouth of a dumb rookie. But Thomas was an established star, the innocent cherub with the big smile, and his image was taking a significant hit.

A tape of the interview was played on WJR-AM in Detroit, confirming Thomas's quote. After he was done speaking, sounds of Thomas laughing could also be heard.

Thomas said the incident was taken out of context, that he was obviously being "sarcastic" in his agreement with Rodman. Thomas said the remarks caused him and his mother much grief, but the controversy soon blew over, mostly due to Bird's goodwill. He staged a press conference with Thomas, absolving the Pistons guard without much concern.

"I don't think Isiah meant it as a racist remark," Bird said. "I like Isiah. I still like Isiah. Besides, he knows I'm bad."

As for Rodman?

"Rodman just talks too much," Bird said.

He and the Pistons had become the conversation piece leading up to the NBA Finals. They were treading beyond the line of sportsmanship, and they were not making any friends.

Especially Rodman.

"There must be a wind tunnel between those ears," Lakers coach Pat Riley said.

Rodman knew he had gone too far. He reported to camp the next season knowing that somehow he had to make amends.

"I regret what I said," Rodman said. "It was one of those things that never should've been said. It caused a lot of commotion. Really, I've said enough."

Yet Rodman continued to evolve on the court. During the postseason, the Pistons had used individual cameras to isolate each member of the opposition. Rodman was entranced by the technology, and studied the tapes for hours. He was becoming highly enlightened for a second-year player, rapidly learning the habits of other forwards around the league. Determined to stay in the league, he studied his own teammates, absorbing everything he could. And he showed up for work as if each day were his last.

"He fought every day in practice," Daly said. "Most teams don't have those type of players. He was full-bore all the time. Every trip down the floor was a challenge to him defensively."

And he also began to understand the art of rebounding. It was a science mastered by Laimbeer, who was a dominating force under the basket despite a lack of quickness and without a hint of jumping ability.

"Coming in, he was a prolific rebounder in college, even though it was a small college in the middle of Podunk, USA," Laimbeer said. "But what he saw in myself was somebody who just wanted the ball, and it was real simple to do because it is. A lot of it is just wanting, moving, sticking your face in there with disregard for your body. That's what he learned—if you stick your face in there, if you work hard, if you're mentally and physically strong, you will get the ball.

"You've got to want it. I wanted the basketball. I learned it was as integral a part of the game as anything else, and Dennis learned that as well."

"Dennis is effective at what he does. He tries to get inside your head and do different stuff."

Karl Malone, Utah Jazz star

Rodman continued to broaden and refine his game, learning how to set crushing screens from Laimbeer and Mahorn, as well as the subtle tricks of latching on to an opponent's arm to prevent him from jumping, or giving a well-timed shove to throw him off-balance.

There was a game inside the game, and Rodman was surrounded with knowledge, lapping up all of the nuances and secrets he could glean.

"I found Dennis to be one of the most intelligent players I've ever been around," assistant couch Brendan Suhr said. "And I've been around some of the most intelligent players in modern-day basketball. I rank him up there—and this will scare some people—as a genius from a basketball standpoint.

"He has great God-given basketball intelligence, and he uses it. He became one of the best screeners in the game; he knows how to put a body on you. He can execute a pick-and-roll as well as anybody who's ever played. And he used to be able to tell me everything about every player's tendencies, their strengths and weaknesses, better than any coach I've ever been around."

Soon, it became impossible to keep Rodman on the bench. In his second season, 1987–88, he averaged over 26 minutes a game, severely cutting into Dantley's playing time.

Late in that season, Dantley sprained his ankle, and Rodman was thrust into the starting lineup. The Pistons were magically transformed into a vicious defensive team. They toppled the rising Bulls 89–74 in Chicago, with Rodman contributing 15 points and 10 rebounds. They played again a few days later at the Silverdome, and Rodman had 15 points and a career-high 19 rebounds in an 82–73 victory.

It was clear to both Daly and Dantley that Rodman made the Pistons more vibrant, and Dantley became disenchanted. Rodman couldn't care less, enjoying his flourishing role. He averaged 11.6 points and 8.7 rebounds off the bench in 1987–88, the last time in his career that his points outnumbered his rebounds over the course of a season.

With the defensive glass stubbornly monitored by Laimbeer and Mahorn, Rodman displayed a profound talent for offensive rebounding. Of his 715 rebounds that season, 44 percent were on the offensive end, the highest ratio he has ever registered.

"He was smart enough to realize he'd never be a scorer in this league."
Chuck Daly

And yet he was surprisingly deficient as a free-throw shooter, the league's worst at 54 percent. The coaching staff was curious about the trend, considering that Rodman had little difficulty in practice.

"He could score, but he didn't have a scorer's mentality," Malone said. "He was knocking down free throws all the time in practice, but when he got into the game, he became self-conscious. He did not want to be at the line."

What the coaching staff uncovered was Rodman's tremendous fear of failure, one that would be painfully reinforced in the 1987–88 playoffs.

That season, the Pistons won their first divisional title since moving to Detroit in 1957, posting a 54-28 record. They had a tough time with the Washington Bullets in the first round of the playoffs, but in the decisive Game 5, Rodman scored 12 of his 13 points in the fourth quarter, leading the Pistons to a 99–78 win and a series victory.

They disposed of the Bulls in five games, and then broke Boston's stranglehold on the Eastern Conference, parlaying a pivotal overtime win in Game 5 at the Garden into a 4–2 series triumph.

They were playing the Lakers in the NBA Finals, and after taking a 3–2 lead in the series were on the brink of breaking a dubious record—the Pistons had existed three decades in Detroit without a championship, one of the longest streaks of futility of any sports franchise in America.

Just as against the Celtics in the conference finals the previous season, the Pistons were on the brink of triumph, only to be denied.

Isiah Thomas was in the midst of authoring one of the most courageous performances ever seen in the NBA Finals, scoring 25 of his 43 points in the third quarter of Game 6, despite badly spraining an ankle midway through the period. And the Pistons held a three-point lead with one minute to play, silencing a stunned crowd in Los Angeles.

But the Lakers fought back, moving to within one on a Byron Scott jumper. Following a Thomas miss, Laimbeer was whistled for a touch foul on Lakers center Kareem Abdul-Jabbar.

Jabbar made both free throws with 14 seconds left, and following a time-out, Joe Dumars missed a potentially game-winning shot.

The Lakers had survived, winning 103–102.

"They had their chance and they knew it," Lakers forward James Worthy said.

In Game 7, Thomas tried to play, but his swollen ankle wouldn't comply. The Pistons valiantly tried to stay in the game, and trailed by only three with under 40 seconds left.

Vinnie Johnson came across halfcourt. Salley was open under the basket, but Johnson made a rare mistake in judgment, instead firing a pass to Rodman, who stood just inside the three-point line. For a moment, Rodman stood motionless, unsure of himself. Not one of the Lakers standing in the paint jumped out to guard Rodman, almost daring him to shoot.

He did.

Clank.

Game over, championship lost. Final score: 108–105, Lakers.

That miss would forever change the way Rodman looked at his offensive game. It was a simple miss, but Rodman felt he had cost the Pistons a championship. It was a simple miss, but it would stick in Rodman's craw, tapping into all his insecurities.

There was only one way to avoid such embarrassment in the future.

Stop shooting the ball.

Rodman returned the next season craving atonement, and his desire was obvious. He was the only veteran to show up at the Windsor camp for rookies and free agents, and decided on a failsafe plan for the upcoming season.

He would abandon the offense, concentrating solely on defense and rebounding.

It was a decision that didn't bother the Pistons coaches at all.

"He looked around the league and and was smart enough to realize he'd never be enough of a scorer to take shots away from Bill

Laimbeer, Vinnie Johnson, Isiah Thomas, and Joe Dumars," Daly said. "It was a brilliant decision."

Said Suhr: "Chuck told all of his players that you can make a hell of a living by doing the little things that no one wants to in this game. If you have a definable NBA skill, you can stay in this league forever. He challenged Dennis to become the best defender in the league, and Dennis took to that."

Midway through the 1988–89 season, the Pistons made a drastic change. They traded Dantley to the Dallas Mavericks in exchange for Mark Aguirre, who was on the downslope of a solid career and had never won a championship.

After his first practice with the Pistons, Aguirre couldn't believe the intensity. Finally, after two hours of banging, he threw up his hands in frustration:

"I have no rights on this team," Aguirre said.

"Anything you get, you earn," Salley replied. "It's the Piston way."

Aguirre was a soft player with a soft touch, but he didn't need the ball as much as Dantley. He was also tight with Thomas from their boyhood days spent together on the Chicago playgrounds, prompting Dantley to publicly criticize the trade.

In reality, the Pistons were simply making room for Rodman.

"From Day One, when Dennis first came to our team, I remember we had an exhibition game against the Celtics," Thomas said. "Bird and I were talking before the game, and I told him that Rodman was going to be a great player.

"The more time he got on the court, the better he became, and the harder it was to keep him off the court. That was the problem. Remember how I got the blame for Adrian Dantley? The problem was Dennis Rodman. You couldn't keep him off the court. How could you justify keeping him out of the game?"

Rodman was now the Pistons' sixth man, but he was playing 27 minutes a game. He averaged 9.4 rebounds and 9.0 points per game, but evolved into something that's hard to quantify.

With quick feet, blazing speed, and long arms, he was able to guard anyone the Pistons requested, including Michael Jordan. While he was still skinny as a rail, he had legs strong as tree trunks. And despite being oversized, the power in his lower body allowed him to defend the bigger forwards in the league and not get steam-rolled.

"He was our X factor," Suhr said. "He was the guy who would go out and stop the other team's best player, and yet, he could still go in there and bang. But he had something else that made him unique, a tremendous pain threshold and reckless abandon with his body, which is unusual for an NBA player."

Rodman did something else that season that he's never done before or since:

He led the league in field goal percentage, shooting .595 from the floor to easily best the 76ers' Charles Barkley (.579). It was, more than anything, evidence of Rodman's finicky approach to offense, his desire to shoot only when the percentages were high, to never miss a big shot again.

He had taken 709 shots the previous season. But in 1988–89, despite an increase in playing time, his shots dipped to 531 and his scoring fell off over two points a game.

"He'd get the ball two feet in front of the basket and dribble out," Laimbeer said. "He just didn't want to go to the foul line, he didn't want to shoot a free throw."

In the Pistons' scheme, it hardly mattered. They were on full-throttle, their rogue image occupying center stage.

They had ripened and matured, compiling a 63-19 record and emerging as the team to beat in the NBA. The trade of Dantley had eased the friction, liberating a group that won 34 of its last 37 games.

"Along with Laimbeer and Mahorn, Dennis came to personify the 'Bad Boy' image."

Phil Jackson, Chicago Bulls coach

They reveled in their role of gloating instigators, leading the league in fines by almost a 3–1 margin. The Pistons were collectively docked $29,100 by the NBA in 1988–89, while the Trail Blazers and Pacers were next at $10,500.

In fact, with $11,000 in fines by himself, Mahorn alone would have led all NBA teams.

Nevertheless, the Pistons thundered through the playoffs. They swept the Celtics 3–0, although Boston was without Bird for the first two games. They next swept Milwaukee, then were stretched to six games by the Bulls, who were slowly closing the gap on the Pistons, driven by the incomparable will of Michael Jordan.

The Bulls won two of the first three games of the series, including the opener in Detroit. But the Pistons got physical, and went on to win the next three games. Pippen injured the arch of his foot, blaming Rodman for stepping on it. And in the decisive contest, Laimbeer nailed Pippen with an elbow to the cheekbone, rendering the Bulls forward unconscious for three minutes.

Rodman led the Pistons with 15 rebounds in Game 6, a 103–94 victory over the Bulls at Chicago Stadium. And at one point, he jumped in and snatched the ball away from Laimbeer, who had already corralled the rebound.

"I just feel that every ball that goes through the rim is mine," Rodman said. "It belongs to me—even if Bill Laimbeer has it. I know when I did it, Laimbeer got ticked off. I said, 'Sorry Bill, but sometimes I get so caught up.'"

Laimbeer understood.

"I used to do the same thing when I first got here," Laimbeer said. "So I just let it go."

After the series was over, Jordan was asked who he was cheering for in the Finals.

"I'd say Los Angeles," Jordan said. "No, wait a minute. Detroit. Yeah, Detroit. I want Detroit to bring the title back to the Eastern Conference."

And then he paused.

"Maybe then they'll be nice guys next season," Jordan said.

On the eve of the Lakers-Pistons rematch in the NBA Finals, Byron Scott went down with an injury. Magic Johnson would be slowed by a hamstring injury. The Lakers were done, their run of domination over. It was time for a new champion, and the Pistons were foaming at the mouth. They destroyed the Lakers, sweeping the four-game series.

Rodman's minutes were down to 24 a game during the postseason, mostly due to severe back spasms he suffered just before the Finals. But nevertheless, he led the team with 10 rebounds a game in the postseason, unseating Laimbeer for the honor. It was, in effect, a very symbolic changing of the guard.

And in his sixth year of organized basketball, after five previous postseasons that ended in nightmare fashion, Rodman was a champion.

For the first time.

"To all those people, I'm just a hot dog while Bill Laimbeer and Rick Mahorn are the Bad Boys," Rodman said. "They say we just do all our antics to tick people off. But if I was playing on their team, I don't think they'd call me a hot dog.

"Look at the Chicago Bears. They made a major turnaround when they got [Jim] McMahon and all those guys. I think that's the same here with us when they got Salley, Joe [Dumars], me, and everybody else. We gave them that fight, and now we're one of the elite teams in the league."

Before the 1989–90 season, the Pistons had a dilemma: with the

Orlando Magic and Minnesota Timberwolves joining the league, they had to sacrifice one of their key players in the upcoming expansion draft.

With Rodman showing the promise of a budding star, they left Rick Mahorn unprotected, and he was scooped up by the Timberwolves.

Rodman was thrust into the starting lineup, but the Pistons only became more formidable on defense. With Mahorn, they were second in the league in defense, allowing 100.8 points per game. With Rodman, they led the league, allowing 98.3 points per game.

By mid-season, Rodman was averaging nine points and nine rebounds a game, but his contributions were undeniable and impossible to discount.

He was selected by the Eastern Conference coaches as an All-Star Game reserve. And later that season, he was named the NBA's Defensive Player of the Year.

"Playing defense was all about pride," Daly said. "It's a macho way to go. People who play defense are macho people, and Dennis liked that image."

Yet when he received the award for top defensive player, there was nothing macho about his reaction. Rodman simply broke down and cried in front of the cameras, surrendering to a moment of complete exhilaration and stunning revelation.

He had fought his way to the top, working for everything he had earned. He had spent the first portion of his career in anonymity. He was the working man's hero in Detroit, where he lived in an apartment complex and mingled with the common folks, but he was just one component of a star-laden team.

But now he had a tangible symbol of respect, a shiny trophy and league-wide appreciation for what he brought to the game.

"We all knew how emotional Dennis was," Daly said. "He was always the most sensitive guy around, one who wore his heart on his sleeve. You have to go all the way back to that rookie camp in Windsor to know what Dennis was feeling. When he was drafted, he wasn't sure that he could play in this league.

"But when he won that award, it was confirmation. He was in awe. He realized, 'Hey, I've got some skill.' "

The Pistons would repeat as NBA champions, but not without an ominous series against the Bulls in the Eastern Conference Finals.

The Bulls stretched the series to seven games, and Daly noticed that the referees were becoming less and less tolerant of the Pistons' physical style. Jordan had publicly complained that the Pistons were not good for the game of basketball, and there seemed to be a movement within the NBA to clean up some of the thuggery and reemphasize the grace.

Daly knew that the Pistons' style had a short shelf-life, that they had to make the most of this run before it was too late.

But in Game 7, the Pistons once again smothered the Bulls. Pippen was invisible, stricken with a severe migraine headache that resulted in a 1-of-10 shooting performance, and the Pistons advanced with a 93–74 victory.

Rodman would later claim that he might have been the reason for Pippen's headache, but one thing was clear:

While the Pistons romped over the Portland Trail Blazers in the NBA Finals, winning the last three games on the road to capture their second championship, their reign was nearing an end.

nine

BITTER END

"Dennis is loyal to people. Not to franchises, organizations, or other nonhuman entities. He's loyal to human beings, and fiercely loyal to his friends."

Dick Versace

Although he was now a two-time NBA champion, Rodman was feeling strangely dejected. He wasn't a dominating force against the Trail Blazers, hampered by a sprained ankle that severely limited his productivity.

In Game 2, the injury sapped Rodman's trademark quickness, and he fouled Clyde Drexler late in the game after being beaten on a drive to the basket. Drexler sank his free throws, leading the Trail Blazers to their only victory of the series.

Daly would rest Rodman in the next two games, and he played only sparingly in the clinching victory.

And he had felt frozen out on offense, purposely ignored in the Pistons' scheme. He thought it started in the Eastern Conference Finals against the Bulls. He thought it continued in the NBA Finals. He felt like a liability when his team had the ball, and was convinced his teammates thought the same.

In all probability, it was a strong case of paranoia, likely stemming from that single miss against the Lakers two years before.

Either way, it was time to carve a stronger identity, to become an irreplaceable force.

It began with shaving slogans into his hair—one game "Cha Ching" would be inscribed on the back of his head, while the next week it might be "Ba Da Bing."

But the heavy emphasis was a crazy passion for rebounding, one that hit fifth gear in the 1990–91 season. He had it all figured out now, the different trajectory that each of his teammates had on their jump shot, how different angles produced different caroms, and how to position himself accordingly.

"He became a rebounding fool," Thomas said.

"All he cared about was winning and rebounding," Malone said. "He became so good at it. He was constantly circling, never taking a direct route to the basket. He was always getting inside his man, and his relentless pursuit to get the basketball is what separated him from everyone else. He would give a third, a fourth, even a fifth effort, tapping the ball to himself. If the ball was on the floor, he would dive for it. He was obsessed with winning a rebounding title."

Rodman had outrebounded Laimbeer the previous season by the slightest margin, 792–780, surpassing a man who had led the Pistons in rebounding the last eight years.

In 1990–91, there was no contest.

Rodman pulled down 1,026 rebounds that season, averaging 12.5 a game, second in the NBA only to San Antonio's David Robinson (13.0). And he was again named Defensive Player of the Year, forging an image as the hardest-working man in the league.

"Nobody taught me how to rebound," Rodman said. "To me, rebounding ain't nothing but desire and hard work. It's pure commitment to a purpose and a role. All I ever did was follow my desire to go to the boards for every rebound as if it's my personal property.

"I'm not what you'd call a high jumper. I'm not strong, and everybody sees that I don't have a big body. But I do have quickness and courage, and I'm not afraid of being banged. I just get in there and go for every rebound.

"You simply have to outwork me. Hard work made me what I am today. I'm not in this league because I'm a great shooter. I don't feel that I'm that great a rebounder, either.

"But it's hard for people to really stay with me because I have such a tremendous work ethic as far as going for the ball. It's mine. It belongs to me coming off the rim. Plus, I do all the little things like playing tough defense, diving after the loose balls, blocking out and setting the picks—all the little things that help us win."

Problem was, the balance of power had shifted in the Eastern Conference. The Bulls had made two shrewd acquisitions in the off-season, acquiring veteran Cliff Levingston and drafting a power forward named Scott Williams. They helped offset the Pistons' edge in size and strength, and coupled with the continuing evolution of Jordan and Pippen, it allowed the Bulls to finally catch up with their rivals.

The Bulls dethroned the Pistons in the Central Division that season, winning 61 games and finishing with an 11-game lead over their nemesis.

The passing of the torch couldn't have been more obvious.

The Bulls swept the Pistons in the Eastern Conference Finals, winning all four games, including the last two on Detroit's home floor. They went on to beat the Los Angeles Lakers in the NBA Finals, embarking on a string of three consecutive championships.

The Pistons were put out to pasture, but not without a fight. They entered the NBA's elite fraternity with bad intent, kicking everyone out until they stood alone at the top. And in symmetrical fashion that put bookends on their reign of terror, the Pistons would leave kicking and screaming.

In Game 4 against the Bulls, the Pistons committed 30 personal fouls and a flagrant foul, and were whistled for four technical fouls. And Rodman once again landed in the NBA's doghouse.

With 7:03 left in the second quarter, Laimbeer committed a hard foul on Pippen as he attempted a layup. After the play was over, Rodman pushed Pippen, who was already off-balance and went tumbling out of bounds. Pippen would need six stitches to close the wound on his chin, and to this day still carries the scar as a reminder of Rodman's cheap shot.

"I'm just a weird individual. Unpredictable. Unbalanced. One minute, I feel one way. Then the next, I feel different. That's just the way I am."

Dennis Rodman

In the closing moments of the Bulls' 115–94 victory, a time-out was called. And in an incredible display of poor sportsmanship, most of the Pistons walked off the floor into the locker room.

Only John Salley hung around to congratulate the Bulls.

Afterward, a visibly angry Rodman again let loose:

"I gave a hard foul," Rodman said. "Nothing wrong with that. I'm glad he's not hurt. But they'd do the same to us.

"I'm hoping the Lakers win. The Bulls have ridiculed us the

whole time. They say we are the dirtiest team in the league, and that we shouldn't be in the league. But since Michael Jordan's, like, the top NBA star, I guess he can say anything he wants to say. So, hey, I'm not giving them anything."

Rodman was then asked if he thought the NBA Finals would be competitive.

"Competitive? Shoot! If they can bitch and complain like they did about us, heck yeah, they'll be all right. They can take the pacifiers out now. Hey, everything's all right. And Phil Jackson had better take that diaper off. Things are starting to look too wet now. It doesn't matter who the Bulls play, the Lakers or Portland, because we're not going for the Bulls. We're not giving the Bulls no credit."

Although Rodman was not called for a foul on the shove he gave Pippen, he was later fined $5,000. There was a league-wide fury directed at the Pistons' behavior, particularly the galling scene of a defeated champion walking off the court without shaking hands.

"Inappropriate," Suhr admitted. "But that team had an insatiable desire to win. There was no individual goals. There was only one thing—winning a championship. If you didn't achieve it, the season was a total failure.

"We were beat by the Bulls, and the players looked at their season as a failure. But they acted inappropriately."

Particularly Rodman, who with his shove of Pippen had crossed the line once again. Only this time, he wasn't a dumb rookie slandering a legend. He was now the NBA's menace, a player who threatened the livelihood of his peers, a player totally out of control.

Even the mayor of Chicago, Richard M. Daley, jumped into the fray.

"They should've fined him $100,000 and the team about a half-million," Daley said. "That's what I would have done."

With intense heat coming from the league, the following fax was sent to Pippen and several news organizations:

I am writing this letter to apologize to you for the incident that happened in Monday's game. You are a great player and I'm glad you weren't hurt by the incident. It was merely one of frustration. I am not the type of player of which I have been accused. The situation was one of those things which should not have happened. I am ready and willing to accept any fines or consequences set by the league for my actions. I sincerely apologize to you, your teammates and the entire Chicago Bulls organization. I also hope there are no hard feelings between you, your teammates and me. Good luck in the NBA Finals—it's a tough road ahead.

Pippen, however, wasn't in the mood for apologies.

"I don't accept his apology because I don't believe Rodman really wrote the letter," Pippen said. "After listening to what he's been saying about the team and the organization for so long, and after what he did to me, it's hard to believe that he has changed completely all at once.

"It was less than a man for him to push me like that. I could've been seriously hurt. Ain't no way for him to cover up the scar. I've received a lot of cheap shots, but his was the lowest blow."

According to Bryne Rich, Rodman wasn't lying. He says he was with Rodman the day he wrote the apology, but it wasn't exactly Rodman's idea.

"He had to sit down and make a note," Bryne said. "He had to apologize. They were really coming down hard on him. He didn't have much of a choice."

The following season, 1991–92, the Pistons tried to claw back, but the magic was gone. Vinnie Johnson was waived in September, and spent the last season of his career with San Antonio. James Edwards was traded to the Los Angeles Clippers for a draft pick. Orlando

Woolridge was acquired in a trade with the idea of offsetting the loss of offense, but the mix wasn't right.

Rodman, however, was spectacular. He played 40 minutes a game and won his first rebounding title, averaging 18.7 rebounds per game. It was the best rebounding performance since Wilt Chamberlain averaged 19.2 per game in 1971–72, and given Rodman's physical stature, it was an amazing accomplishment.

He was named an All-Star for the second time in his career, and this time, played 25 minutes in the contest, yanking down 13 rebounds.

It was another breakthrough season for Rodman, but the seeds of discontent were already growing. The Pistons were overmatched, and while they finished with a 48-34 record, they were mired in third place, 19 games behind the Bulls.

They were eliminated in the first round of the playoffs, losing a five-game series to the New York Knicks.

The dynasty had crumbled. In retrospect, they were two plays away from a string of four championships. They settled for two.

At any rate, it was over, and after the early postseason exit, Daly resigned.

"I was in a position where the team was in decline," Daly said. "They had to look at the coach. They had to look at the team. I was there nine years, which was two years too long. It was time to go. I didn't want to hear them anymore, and they didn't want to hear me. It was never peaches and cream."

Oh, but to Rodman it was.

He had never known his real father, and now the most instrumental man in his life was gone, off to coach the New Jersey Nets.

"Dennis went through what a child goes through in a divorce," Suhr said. "He was terribly broken up by it. It's very rare in this day and age for a player to love his coach, but whenever Dennis was around Chuck, he felt good."

There was also a strange undercurrent of agendas accompanying the change, one that Rodman noticed immediately. He began to loathe the organization he had once loved.

Although Daly and Pistons general manager Jack McCloskey were friends, they had philosophical differences. McCloskey had also fallen in love with the rogue image, going so far as to hire an employee to wave a "Bad Boys" banner around the Palace; Daly wanted to escape the identity, convinced it had caused a backlash from the NBA and, more important, the officials.

McCloskey had also fallen in love with Ron Rothstein, who had served as Daly's assistant from 1986 to 1988. A great strategist, Rothstein had left the organization to become head coach of the Miami Heat, which entered the league in 1988.

Rothstein finished sixth, fifth, and sixth in three years with the Heat before getting fired. And before the 1991–92 season, McCloskey brought Rothstein back, paying him $100,000 to serve as the Pistons' color commentator.

From behind the microphone, Rothstein rarely spoke to Daly during the season, and Rodman took notice. After Daly resigned, Rothstein was moved in as the Pistons' head coach.

To Rodman, Rothstein was a vulture hovering over a carcass. His visions of loyalty were shattered, his family crudely dismembered.

"On the surface, it didn't look like we were that close," Daly said. "But we really were.

"I was like a father figure, I'm sure. There is probably a sense of abandonment on his part because I left the area. And I think there were so many other changes, that he lost a lot of people he felt comfortable with."

Many of those close to the Pistons thought Daly should have been rewarded for bringing two championships to Detroit, that he should have been given a golden parachute in the form of the title of general manager and allowed to rebuild the team in his vision.

Many thought McCloskey had taken too much of the credit. Many felt Isiah Thomas should have received a balloon payment for past services, and that the dismantling of the Pistons was shortsighted.

Rodman thought all of this. And more.

"It was the ugly side of the business," Thomas said. "A lot of us got our hearts broke. When you are as passionate about the sport as we were, the best way to describe it is like a love affair. You give your heart and soul to a woman, and that person breaks your heart."

The change in management gnawed at Rodman all summer, and he had very little to look forward to in the upcoming season. His depression was only enhanced by a disastrous union, an ill-advised marriage that was doomed from the start.

ten
FATAL ATTRACTION

"Somewhere along the way, we lost Dennis."

Bill Laimbeer

With Daly gone, Rodman was devastated.

It was another father who had just disappeared, another divorce that rocked his world. His family within the Pistons' locker room was breaking up, and the pangs of abandonment were beginning to resurface.

There were no anchors left, nobody to lean on.

Except, of course, for Annie.

"An accident waiting to happen," said Matt Dobek, the Pistons' vice president of public relations.

On a spring evening in 1986, Dennis Rodman walked into a Sacramento restaurant after a Pistons-Kings game. He was a rookie enjoying the relish tray of fame, and as soon as he sat down, he was completely enthralled by a gorgeous blond waitress working the floor.

Her name was Anicka Bakes, a twenty-three-year-old model from California. And she would completely change the course of Rodman's life, forever scar his outlook and alter his mind-set.

"He asked me to go back to his hotel room with him," Bakes told *People*. "But I told him I wasn't that kind of girl."

"I'm attracted to white women now and I'm attracted to black women still. But I haven't found a black woman willing to accept me."

Dennis Rodman on the *Oprah Winfrey* show

But the attraction was mutual and obvious, and friends describe the couple as very similar in their quirks and painfully alike in their lack of stability.

They began seeing each other as soon as Rodman's rookie season had ended, and by the summer of 1987, Bakes claims that she and Rodman were living together in his Michigan town house. And she claims they eventually became engaged.

"Dennis was fun to be with," she said. "He has a great sense of humor. And he was gentle. He loved me."

But by the summer of 1988, in an interview with *People*, Bakes said she made a horrible discovery. Two years into their relationship and six months pregnant, Bakes had found evidence that Rodman wasn't exactly monogamous.

When she returned to Sacramento to visit her parents, other women began occupying Rodman's guest seats at the Palace of Auburn Hills. A friend had noticed the strange faces where Annie usually sat, and relayed the information to Bakes. And that wasn't all.

"I would find as many as fifty women's names and telephone numbers written on scraps of paper in Dennis's clothes . . . *in a month*," she said. "I'd come home and find brown hair on our pillows. He'd change the sheets, but my bedspread smelled like perfume."

Bakes said she confronted Rodman with the incriminating evidence, but was met with complete denial. And even after Bakes gave birth to their daughter, Alexis Caitlyn, in the fall of 1988, the relationship remained as tumultuous as ever.

In June of 1989, Bakes decided to go public with the relationship and all its warts. Just as the Pistons were preparing to take on the Lakers in the NBA Finals, Bakes filed a paternity suit in a Los Angeles superior court, detailing charges of abandonment and abuse.

"Dennis Rodman's been playing pro basketball for three years. Now some bimbo comes along and does this."
Rodman's agent, Bill Pollak, in *People* magazine

Bakes claimed that Rodman wasn't so gentle any longer. She cited one incident in which he "forced me to my knees and dragged me on my stomach down a flight of stairs." She claimed that Rodman grabbed her hair and pushed her head into an empty bathtub. She claimed one of their heated arguments concluded with Bakes incurring a badly bruised jaw, and another ended with Bakes "bleeding and crawling into the bathroom" while Rodman pleaded, "I'm sorry. I'm sorry."

She also said in a sworn statement that other than a one-time payment of $1,000, Rodman refused to support his daughter, now eight months old. She petitioned the court for $7,700 a month in child support, $5,000 for Alexis's furniture, and asked for a restraining order to keep Rodman at least one hundred yards away from her home in the Hollywood hills.

She also asked for half of his earnings.

"Because of Dennis's earning ability, Dennis insisted that I stop modeling, and he assured me that he would support me financially with his then-lifestyle and salary," she wrote in the statement filed with the court.

She had hired noted palimony attorney Marvin Mitchelson, who claimed that Bakes was entitled to at least $1 million plus a share of what Rodman would receive from the upcoming NBA Finals. He was setting parameters for a possible settlement, and apparently, that's just what happened. The allegations never made the courtroom, and following the initial splash and the one-sided account in *People*, the case disappeared.

Many years later, Rodman said he could have sued Bakes for the allegations of physical abuse. He didn't but the incident was defused largely because the relationship wouldn't die. They continued their love-hate affair until the summer of 1992, when Rodman made a costly decision.

Maybe, now that Daly was gone, Rodman needed to disappear into the womb of another family—his own. Maybe the situation in Detroit magnified the circumstances with his own daughter, who was now four years old and growing up without the presence of a father. Maybe he simply needed solace, and there was only one place left to find it.

Whatever the reason, Dennis Rodman and Annie Bakes were married before the Pistons reported to training camp.

It lasted eighty-two days.

"They should've never been together," Dobek said. "Annie was worse than Dennis when it came to stability in life. And whenever they got into it, she always played the trump card, which was Alexis."

The marriage, like their cohabitation, was marked by infidelity, which Rodman readily admits in his biography.

"I think Annie did her share of window-climbing and I did my share of door-cracking," he said.

Many sources close to the relationship say the marriage exploded with a horrible twist. And the plot went like this:

She found out about her husband's indiscretions. She became insanely jealous. She extracted revenge by doing the same . . . with one of his teammates. It is one of the most long-standing rumors in the NBA, and if true, one of its worst-kept secrets.

"He was not monogamous," one source said. "She was incredibly jealous so she intentionally committed adultery, and very possibly with someone Dennis knew. These were two very abnormal individuals living a very abnormal relationship."

For Rodman, it all added up to a deep, dark funk. He still had three years left on his contract with the Pistons, but he had no desire to play for Ron Rothstein, no desire to do anything but self-destruct.

He made another costly decision.

He wasn't going to report to camp.

He told the Pistons he was too depressed over his pending divorce and custody battle to play basketball. But in a strange display of

89

arrogance, he showed up as a spectator for the first four exhibition games, watching from a luxury suite.

The Pistons knew they were sitting on a powder keg, and they knew that a rebellion could soon surface around Rothstein. Initially, team president Tom Wilson treated the problem as if he were trying to coax a child out of bed.

"We'd rather not have him here until he's playing because he's becoming a distraction," Wilson said. "Here the team is struggling and the solution to the problem is sitting forty feet away. That's getting to the coaches, who are out there busting their tails. Last year, we won forty-eight games without everybody hating each other. And now, with everybody on the same page, we ought to be better and we would be if the big guy was not sitting in the stands."

Finally, the Pistons got tough. They began fining Rodman $1,000 for every preseason game he missed, and an additional $300 for every practice day that went by without Rodman in camp.

After running up $14,000 in fines and after a long conversation with Daly, Rodman returned to camp.

This time, he had huge tattoos decorating his arm, one bearing the name of his daughter. He had also bulked up significantly over the summer, gaining fifteen pounds in muscle.

But he didn't want to be there. After starting the 1992–93 season with the Pistons, he disappeared again on November 12, and was suspended without pay. He said he was suffering from knee problems, but team doctors wouldn't concur.

He was to earn $2.3 million that year, but amidst Annie's claims that she would try to take as much money from her ex-husband as possible, Rodman had no desire to go back to work. On November 20, he was again suspended without pay, racking up $86,000 in new fines, starting the new season with a lot of bad will and red ink.

Finally, after another chat with Daly, and a summit meeting with the Pistons' hierarchy, Rodman agreed to return.

"I told Dennis, 'You're good for the game. You love the game. It's time to come back,' " Daly said. "I never set out to be a father figure or anything like that to him. I did come to understand that he's a maverick. He's emotional and sensitive. You have to manage him in a certain way."

When Rodman returned, it was like nothing had happened. He put on a uniform, took the court, and dominated like never before. By the middle of December, he was averaging 18.4 rebounds per game, and had an amazing stretch in which he averaged 20 or more rebounds in 12 of 15 games.

All was well, and Rodman conceded as much.

"I know that when I first came back, there was talk that they were showcasing me to trade me," Rodman said. "But since they haven't been able to make any deals, it looks like I'll be finishing the season here, and I don't have any problems with that. I think this is the best place for me anyway. I can play for Rothstein. It's just that I didn't like the way he came in and replaced Chuck Daly.

"It was like a stab in the back, and I would have felt that way about anybody who came in the same way. Chuck and his wife will always be dear to me, and I don't think that was fair to him.

"The way I see it, I'm just playing for my daughter, Alexis, and for the love of the game. Every rebound I grab, every good game I have, I'm doing it all for her. At the same time, being given a second chance by my teammates, I want to do everything in my power to help us win."

It all sounded so nice.

But on January 15, Rodman was sidelined with a torn muscle in his right calf.

And it would become clear that a young man known for his quirks, a man who had lived a lifetime of confusion, had never been so lost, so desperate for attention.

eleven
BIG LIE

"I like to shock people."

Dennis Rodman

ennis Rodman sat in the cab of his truck, staring at the stars, a lost soul alone in the night.

He was deserted and abandoned, all his relationships cracked and floating away in the wind. He was tortured by change, tormented by his broken marriage, and the only tonic was the bullet poised in the chamber of his .22 caliber rifle, cold and indifferent, waiting for a decision.

Open the cover of *Bad As I Wanna Be,* Dennis Rodman's tawdry autobiography, and this is what you find.

On page 1, Dennis Rodman is ready to take his own life, ready to end the misery with a simple squeeze of the trigger:

"On an April night in 1993 I sat in the cab of my pickup truck with a rifle in my lap, deciding whether to kill myself."

Four pages later, he arrives at the brink:

"As I sat there, I thought about my whole life, and how I was ready to cash it all in. Just pull the trigger, bro, and give it to somebody else. Pass on all those problems."

At that moment, Rodman claims to have been struck by a moment of truth, undergoing a complete metamorphosis. He decided to shed the skin of conformity, and adhere to the unconventional twinges he had suppressed for many years. He put the gun down, and walked away that night determined to live in accordance with his own views of self-expression, to satiate his own desires.

Even Barbara Walters seemed conned. In an interview with Rodman on *20/20,* she asked with genuine concern about the night he claimed to have "killed the imposter."

"I was always a follower," Rodman told Walters. "It was like someone grabbed your arm and said, 'Okay, this is your new life now.' "

"That whole thing about Dennis claiming to kill himself was ridiculous. He was just lonely, plain and simple."

Shirley Rodman

93

In reality, this is one of the great Rodman fictions, a sensational ploy designed for one purpose: shock value. It is a giant myth: a man who allegedly confronted his mortality, stared death in the face, only to walk away enlightened by discovery.

It is a good story, a shrewd attempt to enhance the image of a man-child that no one will ever understand.

It is the big lie.

On the evening of February 11, the Bloomfield Township Police Department received a call from Sheldon Steele, a man who was staying at Rodman's house. The friend was concerned over Rodman's mental state, noting that he had seemed despondent for the past few days. He also noticed that Rodman's shotgun was missing, and the equation could lead to suicide.

The call resulted in a bizarre late-night search for Rodman. The information was loaded on the Law Enforcement Intelligence Network with the tag "BOL"—be on lookout—advising all officers in southeast Michigan to watch for Rodman's well-known truck.

A security guard working the overnight shift at the Palace had heard of the report, and noticed Rodman's truck in the loading zone of the arena. He called the Auburn Hills police department, and somewhere around 5:00 A.M., Sergeant Scott Edwards arrived on the scene.

"I seem to recall the whole thing was about this white girl in Farmington who had dumped him. He was despondent about some sort of relationship problems."
Sergeant Scott Edwards

He approached Rodman's truck and found a man apparently asleep behind the wheel.

"I wouldn't have described him as despondent," Edwards said.

"The impression I got from his roommate is that he would do harm to himself, but [Rodman] pretty much denied that stuff.

"His roommate was definitely worried, but [Rodman] downplayed the incident to us.

"I think he was acting like he was sleeping. I don't think we had to wake him. For some reason, the Palace security people were afraid to approach him, but they must have been circling the truck like crazy. I don't think he ever admitted to us that he was contemplating suicide. In fact, he conveyed to us quite the opposite."

Matt Dobek, the Pistons' vice president of public relations, was awakened near 6:00 A.M. and told that they had found Rodman sleeping in his truck in the Palace parking lot. Dobek rushed to the stadium and found a rather embarrassed Rodman.

"I've read his book, where Dennis says he had the gun in his hand," Dobek said. "That's not true. There was no gun in his hand. The gun was in the back of his truck, not even in the cab."

Dobek and the police accompanied Rodman into the Pistons' locker room, where they phoned his agent, Bill Pollak. It is a state law in Michigan that if you are deemed suicidal, you can't be released by the police until you have proved you are no longer a risk to yourself. Thus it was mandated that Rodman must be taken to a psychiatric ward immediately.

Rodman wasn't too keen on that idea, and he and his agent came up with a better one. Rodman would be released into Dobek's custody, and the two would immediately visit Rodman's personal psychiatrist, who lived in Bloomfield Hills.

"Dennis had to leave his truck there, so we get in my car to find this psychiatrist's house," Dobek said. "We had this entourage following us—all the television and radio stations had arrived and were going live with reports.

"Dennis tells me to ditch the media, so I'm driving like a maniac, like an idiot. It's something out of a movie. I look over, and Dennis is asleep."

He eventually lost the trail of reporters, and while Rodman was in dreamland, Dobek's cellular phone began to ring.

It was Dobek's mother, and she had seen the reports, the mad caravan of cars rushing toward Bloomfield Hills. She was concerned over her son's well-being.

"She asked if Dennis was going to shoot me," Dobek said. "In retrospect, it was hysterical."

They arrived at the psychiatrist's house, and after a conversation with Rodman, the doctor shook his head in confusion.

"This is the same Dennis that I know," he told Dobek. "It doesn't seem like anything is wrong to me, and there's certainly nothing to be alarmed about. You can take him home."

They reached Rodman's house at 11:00 A.M., and Dobek escorted him in.

"One thing I did find—and take—was a box of ammunition sitting on the ledge leading into the family room," Dobek said. "Dennis lives on a lake, and we found out from his roommate that they were shooting the gun around the previous night."

It just so happens that Chuck Daly was arriving in Detroit that day, his first return to the Palace since resigning from the Pistons. The Nets were scheduled to play the Pistons the following day, but had come to town early.

Coincidence?

Hardly.

Daly had heard about the incident, and phoned Dobek. Together, they returned to Rodman's house at 2:00 P.M.

"He's a very sensitive guy, and he was very down," Daly said. "I don't think there was ever any thought process of using the gun on himself. I think he wanted attention."

During the conversation, Rodman told his former coach how miserable he was in Detroit, that he didn't like the new coach, that it was terrible without Daly being around, that he wanted to quit basketball.

Daly soothed Rodman, telling him that there were only six weeks left in the regular season, that everyone loses interest at some point, that he needed to play out the string and hope for a trade.

"I told him he only had thirty games left to get through, and that he could be pretty confident that he wouldn't have to be in Detroit the following year," Daly said. "After that, I made little contributions in helping him get through the year."

Later that night, the Pistons held a homecoming party for Daly. Rodman showed up like nothing had happened.

"He went from being suicidal in the morning to eating ribs with Daly that night," Dobek said. "It was vintage Dennis."

Dobek later found a fitting explanation for Rodman's presence in the parking lot. He had worked out at a local gym in Rochester from 2:00 to 4:00 A.M., and decided not to risk going home.

"My assumption is that Dennis knew if he went home he would sleep in and miss practice and get fined," Dobek said. "So he came to the Palace, parked his truck, and went to sleep. He knew that the trainer would see him on his way to work, wake him up, and everything would be fine.

"He wasn't crazy. He wasn't suicidal. My personal opinion is that his friend made the phone call, and Dennis just played along, and down the road, played it up."

And yet it was a turning point in Rodman's life. For after the incident, after noticing the attention he garnered that chaotic evening, Rodman found his reputation instantly magnified. He was desperate for attention, and with a little bit of orchestration, it came in waves.

It was the moment he started to realize the value of being outrageous.

The organization was now a prisoner to Rodman's antics, and they wouldn't end. And when the fines came, he didn't care.

He returned to the team, but the final few months were more of the same. When the trading deadline passed without a deal, Rodman shaved "Bite the Melon" into his hair, a saying that became so popular in Detroit that it was featured on T-shirts frequently seen at the Palace.

He missed a flight after a fight with his ex-wife. He showed up for a game just fifteen minutes before tip-off, claiming he had gotten sick on his way to the Palace and had to stop at three different service station restrooms. And after missing a third practice just three weeks after returning from his calf injury, Rodman was once again suspended for chronic violations of team policy.

Rodman hung around long enough to win another rebounding title, amassing an 18.3 average in 62 games. But he kept tweaking management in the process, further alienating himself from the team.

"The dismantling of the team caused him a lot of problems," Laimbeer said. "But if you're a professional, you do your job. Dennis was called on for more leadership, and he struggled with that. It was his turn to step up and take the younger players into the next five to eight years. But Dennis just likes to show up, bust his ass, play hard, and go home. He's not going to think out the leadership. He's a great soldier, but he wasn't capable of being a lieutenant.

"But all of that stuff that was going on should not impact the way you do your job. He had other people counting on him, and he let them down."

Rodman was still in a Pistons uniform, but he was gone. The team couldn't reach him, and they couldn't get rid of him soon enough.

"He came back reluctantly," said Pistons assistant Brendan Malone. "He was very quiet, very introspective, and he didn't want to talk to anybody. He had built a barrier around himself, and he made it clear he wanted out of Detroit."

The Pistons finished 40–42 that season, missing the playoffs for the first time in ten years, and they missed out by one game. When Rodman decided to play in December, the Pistons were 11–3. During the 14 games he missed by injury, they had gone 3–11.

No one in their right mind blamed Rodman for his missed shot in the 1988 NBA Finals, but in 1992–93, his final season with the Pistons, it's clear that—justified or not—Rodman's absence, both mentally and physically, cost his team a berth in the playoffs. And so deep were his feelings of betrayal, he couldn't care less.

Fresh out of college, he had landed in the eye of the storm, jumping into the mad fury of a team burning to win. And within three years, he was a two-time NBA champion.

He dug himself a trench in the NBA, a man smart enough to specialize, thereby sustaining his career. His abilities were limited, but they were well polished, perfected through intense study and hard work. And by his fourth season, he had emerged as an awesome force, becoming a two-time All-Star and two-time NBA Defensive Player of the Year.

He had forged a tenuous partnership with fame, throwing around money and words with reckless abandon. And when a great dynasty began crumbling at his feet, he was despondent, smothered by a deep depression.

The good years put an indelible stamp on Rodman's psyche. He joined a team bursting with personality. He marveled at the leadership of Isiah Thomas, the quiet professionalism of Joe Dumars and Vinnie Johnson. Like an eager apprentice, he learned the shrewd and crude tricks of Bill Laimbeer and Rick Mahorn.

He played for a coach who extended to his players an enormous amount of freedom. He played for a team that resembled a street gang, offering the kind of reputation that Rodman craved.

They were the Bad Boys, a team of free-spirited thugs, collective masters of the hard foul. They were loathed like no other team in NBA history, accused of smearing a game that once stood for eloquence and grace.

They were hated, but the hatred stemmed from fear and respect. For every game was war, and they knew that on most nights, the other team was an unwilling participant.

They were rebels and rogues, and Rodman fit in perfectly.

And stemming from the furor they caused and the havoc they wreaked, they changed the face of professional basketball.

"He loved what we stood for," Daly said. "He loved how hard we played, that the whole focus was on winning and nothing else."

For Rodman, it was a blessing and a curse. He arrived just when the Pistons were maturing, and could never realize the magnitude or difficulty of his team's ascent into the NBA elite.

He would carry the same expectations into the remainder of his career, and they were both unrealistic and unfair.

For the Pistons were an anomaly, a deep collection of talent and brawn that simply combusted like no team had ever done before. They had their window, but such an inflammatory style of play could never last over the long haul.

"We were all the brothers that he never had," Thomas said. "And we were the last of the gladiator teams. We were the last of that rough-and-tumble era, and Dennis is a throwback, a gladiator, a warrior. That's where his heart is.

"The Pistons organization doesn't stand for what we stood for anymore. We stood for something else, something you rarely see in sports. If you put all of us together, if you were to get myself,

Laimbeer, Mahorn, Vinnie, and Joe together in a room and cut us open, that's what we would bleed.

"The personality of that team and the changes of that era were so complex and diverse, and it made for one of the most interesting times in the history of the NBA. That left a mark on Dennis.

"Dennis is a Piston. And he always will be."

But as the dark days of the 1992–93 season drew to a close, there was only bitterness toward an organization that had fostered Rodman like the misfit he was. The Pistons had run their course, hit the wall, and the glory days were over. And for Rodman, one bad year, one messy divorce, and one big change in management had ruined everything.

Rothstein was fired after the season.

Rodman waited for a new address.

twelve
SPUR OF THE MOMENT

"I love to have a good time and maybe do weird
things, and I don't care what people say. I'm in my
own world."

Dennis Rodman

Dennis Rodman sat in a room in San Diego, listening to the promises, saying as little as possible.

Also in attendance at the confidential meeting were John Lucas, new head coach of the San Antonio Spurs, a former drug addict who had turned his life around; Bob Bass, general manager of the San Antonio Spurs; and a representative from agent Bill Pollak's office, who had accompanied Rodman to the meeting.

On the phone was Bob Coleman, president of the Spurs.

And they were all trying to soothe the fire in Rodman's head.

Rodman had three years left on an $11.8 million contract with the Pistons, and was meeting with the Spurs before giving his blessing on a proposed trade.

But Rodman wanted a commitment to the future. Given his incredible rebounding numbers over the previous two seasons, Rodman not only felt underappreciated, but he was locked in at $2.4 and $2.5 million over the last two years of his deal, and felt tremendously underpaid as well.

He wanted assurance from the Spurs that he would be rewarded financially, but this was a problem.

In the previous collective bargaining agreement between the NBA and the Players Union, there was a clause referred to as the "Over 35" rule. If a player would be over thirty-five years of age when his contract ended, which was the case with Rodman, any extension to that contract would be immediately rolled back into the Spurs' current payroll.

It was a rule designed to prevent teams from circumventing the salary cap by back-loading a contract, basically paying an aging star in the twilight of his career as a reward for his immediate production.

"We thought Dennis was going to be a great, great acquisition."
Bob Bass, former Spurs general manager

Problem was, the Spurs didn't have that kind of room in their payroll to accommodate Rodman's wishes.

But they wanted Rodman badly. And during that meeting, Rodman and his camp insist that the Spurs promised to grant him a one-year extension the following season.

For six million dollars.

Of course, such a commitment would be a violation of NBA policy. Nevertheless, it is a common practice in the league.

In return, Rodman promised he would show the Spurs how to win, and promised to be a team player from start to finish.

And that ended the bumbling, stumbling saga of trading Dennis Rodman.

When the previous season ended, Don Chaney had replaced Rothstein in Detroit, and Rodman again ripped the move. He complained that Brendan Malone should have been given the job, and his constant sniping was not making negotiations easy.

Billy McKinney, then the Pistons' vice president of operations, had gotten so irate with Rodman that he had threatened to keep him in Detroit simply out of spite. He was not operating with maximum leverage.

Rodman had asked to be traded to a warm-weather climate, and the Pistons opened discussions with the Phoenix Suns. The prospect of playing on the same front line as Charles Barkley greatly appealed to Rodman, and Suns president Jerry Colangelo did everything he could to seal the deal.

On four separate occasions, a trade was close to fruition. One package had Rodman going to the Suns for Oliver Miller, Cedric Ceballos, and Negele Knight. But the Pistons had developed a fondness for a young player named Richard Dumas, and after much mixing and matching, an agreement was almost at closure.

Then Dumas suffered a relapse, and was required to undergo therapy for substance abuse. The negotiations were suddenly on tenuous ground.

"I vividly remember our staff interviewing Dennis at the predraft camp in Chicago," Colangelo said. "We knew he was a great athlete who had a real heart, the kind that separates great rebounders from guys who go through the motions.

"We had a real interest in him, but like everyone else, we weren't willing to take a shot at him with a first-round pick. Now, there was an opportunity to get him, and once again, people around the league were real suspect of Dennis. But we were relying heavily on the input of his agent, and we felt we had additional insight to Dennis's behavior, personality, and character.

"The bottom line is, we were prepared to take him. We didn't walk away from it. The other side did."

One theory that surfaced had other general managers around the league desperate to taint the negotiations, acutely aware of how a front line of Rodman and Barkley would completely change the power structure in the West. Sources say that McKinney was given bad information about the players being offered by Phoenix, and after Dumas's unexpected drug relapse, the Pistons abruptly cut off all dialogue with the Suns.

They turned to San Antonio, and on October 1, they struck a deal. The Piston would ship Rodman and Isaiah Morris in return for Sean Elliott and David Wood.

"When we went to San Diego to meet Dennis, I was really impressed by his knowledge of the game and his thoughts on how to defend different players in the league," Bass said. "That prompted us to make the deal. We really needed a power forward, and it was really an outstanding deal for us."

It was certainly a risky acquisition, given Rodman's behavior in Detroit. But the Spurs felt comfortable that Lucas would create an environment allowing Rodman to flourish.

Lucas had never coached a game of basketball in his life when he was signed by San Antonio. But he had beaten his own dark past, overcoming an NBA career marred by four drug-related suspensions, and had dedicated his life to helping others. Before venturing into coaching, he had opened a drug therapy clinic in Houston, and seemed to be just the type who could understand and nurture Rodman.

"When he first came [to San Antonio], I said, 'Dennis, tell me the hoops you want to jump through and I'll tell you the hoops I need you to jump through. Let's reach a common ground.'" Lucas said.

"He said he didn't like shoot-arounds [on the morning of a game]. I told him he would not have to do anything as long as he at least showed up. So we got that out of the way.

"Next thing was dress code. He said he didn't like to wear suits and ties. I said, 'Well, just lace your shoes up because we charter everywhere we go anyways.'

"The third thing I told him is, 'I don't care what color your hair is as long as I don't have to do mine [the same color]. He said, 'Fine.'"

Lucas had set very loose parameters for Rodman, who on the surface seemed far different from the player who had accumulated an impressive highlight film over the past seven years. He had become more than an avid bodybuilder, and his gonzo commitment to spending half his waking hours in the weight room had added another 15 pounds of muscle to his frame. He now weighed 218 pounds, and the difference was easily discernible.

So, too, was his new look.

Before reporting to camp, he wanted to divorce himself from an identity that had carried him through the first phase of his career. When he first joined the Pistons, Rodman had no idea of how to act around established NBA stars, so he snuggled into the background, trying to fit in as smoothly as possible. As he grew in stature, he found that role to be restrictive, but struggled to express his individuality. And when he did, he had found himself chastised and punished.

He craved a new look and a new form of respect, so one day he walked into Olga's Salon in San Antonio. The customers and employees gawked at the celebrity who just ambled through the front door, and Rodman was assigned to a stylist named Fred Baldarrama.

"He was ready to do something crazy, something drastic," Baldarrama said. "We sat down, and he said, 'Why don't we shave it all off and make it blond?' "

Baldarrama complied, and when he was done, Rodman stared in the mirror.

"A big grin came across his face," Baldarrama said. "He said, 'Oh my God, I can't believe I did this.'

"But he wasn't what he seemed to be on the court. He wasn't real wild or anything like that. He was really a quiet guy who kept to himself. He was just doing it to be showy, outrageous, to freak people out."

When he reported to camp, his new teammates stared at him in bewilderment, wondering what had prompted Rodman to change his image so drastically. But once he took the court, it was impossible to take their eyes off him.

Just like he wanted.

He had a new beginning, and for the most part, seemed happy and ready to begin the second phase of his career.

"Yeah, but I won't be completely happy until I can get back with my daughter Alexis," Rodman said at the time. "In the meantime, they appreciate me here, and I feel good about that."

Rodman was then asked about the change in hair color:

"People always want to know what the hell is up with Dennis Rodman," he said. "They say. 'You a crazy nut or what? They think I'm a weirdo. I don't care. I'm going to be me. If you don't like me, to hell with you. I like to show the wildness, the puzzle that is Dennis Rodman.

"Just when you've got me figured out, the next thing you know—boom!—there's something else. I've got a beast in me running wild."

A beast that served only one master, and that was Dennis Rodman.

He immediately reverted to bad habits, showing up late for practice, blowing off shoot-arounds entirely. But in one of his first games for the Spurs, David Robinson poured in 43 points and Rodman set a franchise record with 29 rebounds.

The Spurs knew the combination could be awesome, with Rodman offering the toughness, intensity, and maniacal work ethic that the team sorely needed. The Spurs had finished 49-33 the previous season, but collapsed in the conference semifinals, losing to Phoenix.

Now they were envisioning a championship lineup, and the Spurs hierarchy held their breath, crossed their fingers, and hoped that Lucas knew what he was doing.

One of the early moments that foreshadowed the bumpy road ahead came on November 20, when the Spurs traveled to play the Pistons. It would mark Rodman's first return to Detroit, and the results were strangely predictable.

Earlier in the season, some of the Pistons, most notably Chaney and McKinney, had expressed much relief that Rodman was gone from the organization. Chaney, in particular, stated that Rodman had "overstayed his welcome." Rodman came into the game seething, and was clearly out of control.

He was ejected from the game after receiving two technical fouls. One was for shoving Laimbeer, one of his mentors. The other was for shoving Elliott, the man he was traded for.

Rodman had 8 points and 14 rebounds when he was tossed, and the Spurs lost, 95–86. After the game, Rodman took his ire out on the Pistons crowd.

"If I had my way, I wouldn't have come back here at all," Rodman said. "The fans are two-faced. They forget that I helped bring two championships here. Other guys return and they are welcomed back. They treated me like I'm the worst guy in the world."

In early December, the Spurs acquired Jack Haley, a veteran center who, like Rodman, had never played high school basketball, picking up the game in college.

"When I walked into the locker room, our lockers were side by side," Haley said. "I said, 'Hey, how are you doing, man?' He didn't acknowledge my presence. He didn't say hello. He didn't shake my hand. We didn't speak for about a month. I noticed he never spoke to anybody."

Finally, Rodman trusted Haley enough to allow him inside his small circle of friends. He asked Haley and his wife to go out for a drink one night, and Rodman took the couple to one of his favorite places: San Antonio's most rocking gay/alternative nightclub.

Once inside, Haley played along. He slipped a dollar bill into the G-string of one of the club's dancers, and Rodman knew he had found a kindred spirit.

"I shocked him," Haley said. "We got along fairly well from there."

They would slowly form a solid alliance, a friendship built on a mutual trust shared by two outsiders. They shared an affinity for Las Vegas, and by Haley's recollection, the two made nineteen trips to the city in one year. Haley would become Rodman's confidant, and as much as he could, tried to help Rodman keep his perspective.

For when he was focused, Rodman was brilliant. He strung together a stretch of six games that amounted to a rebounding clinic, five in which he totaled more than 20 rebounds.

But in a game against the Bulls in December, Rodman lost control once again. He head-butted the Bulls' Stacey King, nearly inciting a riot. King responded by pushing Rodman in the face, and both would be heavily fined by the league.

Rodman earned a one-game suspension and a $7,500 fine. King was also suspended for one game, and docked $2,500.

"Most people told me they had wished I had punched him in the face and knocked him out," King said.

Rodman said his motivation was simply a lack of motivation on the part of his teammates.

"We needed a jolt in the ass," Rodman said. "So I did it to try and motivate us. If I got thrown out because of a head-butt, then this league has problems. People hold and grab me, but they don't see that. It's getting bad, to the point where you can't touch anybody. You've got to stand up for what you believe in."

So did Lucas, who knew there was dissension building among his players. The head-butting incident was Rodman's first malicious act as a member of the Spurs, and his teammates were beginning to doubt his commitment and reliability.

"I told Dennis it was my job to motivate the team," Lucas said. "I know Dennis has to stick up for himself, but we also need him in the game. I don't anticipate this happening again."

Yeah, right.

Less than two weeks later, Rodman was ejected in a game against the Los Angeles Lakers. He engaged in an argument with some of the fans, and was later fined $10,000 for refusing to leave the court.

In a team meeting after the game, some of the players read the riot act to Rodman.

"It was a team thing and we all said something," David Robinson said. "His [argument with the fans] bothered me."

Of course, the chastising only made Rodman withdraw even further, convinced he was being unfairly accused, blamed for all of his team's problems.

There would be good times when his courage was inspirational, like the night Rodman suffered a deviated nasal septum after being elbowed in the nose by the Dallas Mavericks' Popeye Jones. Despite missing more than five minutes with a bloody nose that game, an injury that would eventually require surgery, Rodman finished with 32 rebounds.

There would be strange times, like the day in Boston when a fan phoned Rodman in his hotel room and asked if he would dye his hair green in tribute to his beloved Celtics. Rodman agreed, but only if the fan paid him $100,000, which would be donated to charity.

And there was an unforgettable interview with Roy Firestone on ESPN's *Up Close.*

It would be Rodman's first taste of national exposure as a solo act, his first cross-country forum since forging an image as the crazy hired gun paid to pump life into the San Antonio Spurs.

Firestone had had Rodman on the program a few years earlier, intrigued by the story of a young black man who picked up basketball in college, and somehow ended up sharing a home with a white ranching family. Now Rodman had evolved into a wild child, and Firestone knew it would make good copy.

They met in San Antonio, and when Rodman walked into the room, Firestone wanted to go over some parameters:

"I say, 'Dennis, today I want to . . .'" Firestone said. "But he interrupts me and says, 'Listen, you ask me anything. I have a lot to say.' I told him it might turn into a real shrinklike affair, and he said, 'I don't fucking care. The league just wants to fuck me.' So I tossed my notes and decided to push it."

In the first part of the interview, Rodman said he had given away over $35,000 to homeless people, a tab accumulated from his practice of rolling down his window at a stoplight and throwing money at a stranger. He also said he had squandered every penny he earned at the tables in Las Vegas, the result of some strange death wish, a desire to see it all just come and go.

The second part began with Firestone debunking a myth:

Firestone: I want to go back to the incident at the Palace at Auburn Hills, four-thirty or five-thirty in the morning, whatever it was. This is the report we got, you tell me what really happened: "He had a gun. It was loaded. He had his pickup truck and he was fixin' to think about maybe blowing himself away. He was suicidal. He was crazed. He was going to do something bad at five-thirty in the morning in the parking lot of the Palace at Auburn Hills." What happened?

Rodman: That sounds good, don't it?

Firestone: Yeah.

Rodman: That's a picture right there, boy.

Firestone: Is it close?

Rodman: Oh no. It's not close at all. It's not close. They want to sell papers so I guess they can say what the hell they want to say.

Firestone: What's the truth?

Rodman: The truth is I do what I do all the time. I leave at two to three in the morning, ride around, listen to some music, maybe go work out at four or five in the morning. But that time right there I just chilled in the parking lot.

Firestone: But why with a loaded shotgun?

Rodman: A twenty-two? I'd have to shoot myself a hell of a lot of times to kill myself with a twenty-two.

Later in the interview, Firestone decided to get personal:

Firestone: What do you like about the way you look?

Rodman: Nothing.

Firestone: Nothing?

Rodman: Nothing.

Firestone: You don't like the way you look? You couldn't do the hair the way you do if you didn't care about the way you look. Come on, now.

Rodman: You know what's the amazing thing, though? I can be the ugliest guy in the world, [but] if I have lots of money, I can get anybody I want. It makes a lot of sense, don't it? I'm not the most attractive guy in the world, but I have a lot of things that people want to see and people want to read. I'm very interesting to a lot of people.

Firestone: How about Madonna? Recently, we read that Madonna thought you were a turn-on. Would you like to meet Madonna? Would you like to spend any time with Madonna? Does she turn you on?

Rodman: Aw, shit. Be her material boy?

Firestone: *(laughs)* Material boy, huh?

Rodman: Imagine that, huh? No, Madonna . . . I think she likes me because I'm kind of on the weird side, just like her."

Firestone: On the edge?

Rodman: I'm very much on the edge.

Firestone: Is she your type?

Rodman: Is she my type? I don't know. Depends how she is in bed.

Firestone: Ooooh. Can we ask you a little about that?

Rodman: I don't care. Ask me anything.

Firestone: Okay, what's it like, an evening with Dennis?

Rodman: You've got to go with the flow, spur of the moment, you got to go at it. You can't hesitate. Whatever hits you in your mind, you better pursue it.

Firestone: Are you responsible sexually?

Rodman: No.

Firestone: You're not?

Rodman: I don't like sex like most people think I do, because I'm an athlete. That's not the case.

Firestone: You practice safe sex?

Rodman: I've got a girlfriend, so it's basically that we get together and get solid, so, you know, I'm with her, it's a wonderful thing. With anybody else . . . Madonna? I don't know about that. I guess I could dream about that.

Firestone: What if she calls you after she saw this?

Rodman: I don't think she'll be calling me.

Firestone: Will you take the call?

Rodman: I'll take it, see what the hell is going on. My girlfriend [will] say, "Oh, Madonna, she wants to get with you." I say. "Bring her on. I'm ready to get solid." I won't sleep with her, but I'll see what the hell she's talking about.

As the interview neared conclusion, Firestone decided to get personal, pushing the depth of Rodman's vulnerability. He asked Rodman to put all the hyperbole aside, and disclose what really matters to him:

Rodman: I have this area that I just don't want nobody to get into. I don't want nobody to get around Dennis Rodman. I just have those demons inside of me. Stay away. But I do love to help people. I do care about a lot of things.

Firestone: I'll tell you one of the things you care about. You care about children. Doc Rivers spent an afternoon . . . I think with his little girl, and you connected with this little child better than anyone has ever connected. And somebody said were it not for children, Dennis Rodman would be completely alone in the world because children are the only kinds of people who really relate to him, really understand.

Rodman: Boy, that sounds like a little story we heard about Michael Jackson, isn't it? Something like that, isn't it?

Firestone: It's not to that extent, perhaps. But, seriously, is that true about children? [That] they find something inside of you that no one else can find?

Rodman: I think the reason why really I relate to children is because of my child. I think because I don't see my daughter, so when I see a little girl . . .

Suddenly, Rodman is choked up. He tries to speak, but is prisoner to the bulging lump in his throat. He is wearing sunglasses, but the tears begin streaming toward his mouth. There is an awkward yet poignant silence for the next twenty-two seconds.

Firestone: What is it? What is it that touches you about your little girl?

Rodman: I just think that I don't get to see her.

Firestone: You could pick up the phone and call her.

Rodman: I have done that many times, but for some reason, I just can't get through, you know? I just think that whenever I see kids and I hear girls, children laughing and laughing . . . it's kind of hard that I don't get that in my . . . that I don't get to hear . . . that I don't get to hear my daughter do all of those things.

Firestone: Is that, to you in your life, the one failure you've had? That you can have all this success and fame and not being able to have your child around for whenever you can find the time to be with her? I mean, you've been criticized for not having enough time, but when you do have the time to be around her, that's the failure. She's not there and you can't be with her and you've failed in that way?

Rodman: A lot of people say I have [failed], but that doesn't mean I'm a bad person. Doesn't mean I haven't done my job.

Firestone: How do you say—and this is TV, this is theatrics, this is nonsense—How do you say "I love you" to your little girl?

Rodman: Well, I figure that she will know in the future. That's why I put the tattoo on my arm because I feel like when she gets old enough, she'll realize. She may not understand now, but when I see her and she's older at least I can tell her that there were some problems early in her life, that I couldn't be there, that it was a situation where me and her mother couldn't get along. But she can always know that I love her, and she'll always be with me, no matter what.

After the interview, Rodman told friends he wished he hadn't broken down on national television, complaining that it made him seem like a wuss. Others thought the crocodile tears were all part of a staged performance, even though it would take an accomplished thespian to produce that kind of emotion on cue.

But it was clear to all that Rodman was a troubled soul, and surely, there would be trouble ahead.

There was.

In March, he was fined $5,000 for head-butting Utah's John Stockton. He was later ejected from successive games, and for an encore, missed a flight from San Antonio to Houston. He arrived twenty-minutes before tip-off, and in a rare show of discipline from Lucas, spent most of the game seated on the floor near the end of the bench.

Near the end of the third period, Rodman tried to get Lucas's attention by holding up a towel in which he had scribbled the following message: "I'm sorry. Can I play? Please."

It was typical Rodman behavior, the kind that made it nearly impossible to harbor any deep-rooted anger toward him.

But that was beginning to change.

By the middle of March, Rodman had twenty-eight technical fouls, five ejections, and two one-game suspensions. The NBA had had enough of his antics, and called Rodman on the carpet.

He and Lucas were summoned to a private meeting with NBA

commissioner David Stern, who lectured Rodman about his unending penchant for trouble.

Rodman, according to insiders, also used the forum to vent on Stern, telling the commissioner that he was ruining the game by "taking it where you can't be bad boys anymore."

After the meeting, Stern had this to say:

"I reviewed with Dennis Rodman his conduct in a number of San Antonio Spurs games, and we had a frank and open discussion about the responsibilities of an NBA player on the court. I have also made it clear that if a player exhibits a pattern of inappropriate behavior on the court, his coach and team will ultimately be held accountable."

Rodman and Lucas went directly from the meeting to Denver for a game against the Nuggets. And just hours after the conference, Rodman drew his twenty-ninth technical foul. He was now wearing a plastic face mask to protect his nose, and after the technical, he hurled the mask at the Spurs' bench.

Lucas quickly yanked Rodman from the game, and the crowd booed.

Not Rodman, but Lucas.

A dangerous precedent was being set. Rodman had become consumed with self-promotion, constantly changing his hair color and playing to the fans. He had become an icon to the Mexican-American fan base in San Antonio, and the more his volatile nature surfaced on the court, the more the fans responded.

"I've learned to let people be who they are as long as they're doing what they're supposed to do," Lucas said. "But I didn't know his behavior of being an irritant on the court was going to make him a star."

Lucas, however, stuck to his instincts. He was certainly a different breed of coach, allowing his players unprecedented freedom, including the ability to set some of the team rules and call their own plays. During time-outs, he was known to walk to midcourt and prop himself up against the scorer's table, allowing his players to gather themselves without instructions from the coaching staff. He was preaching self-reliance and accountability, and despite the unorthodox methods, Lucas was rarely questioned.

The Spurs won 55 games in Rodman's first season, just three games behind Houston, which won the Midwest Division. Rodman won his third consecutive rebounding title, averaging 17.3 rebounds per game. Despite his growing persona, he stayed in the lineup for 79 games, averaging nearly 38 minutes a contest.

And when David Robinson poured in 71 points in the final game of the season, he surpassed Shaquille O'Neal for the scoring title. It marked the first time in history that a pair of teammates combined to win the scoring title and rebounding title in the same season.

"There was a lot of media attention focused on Dennis, and a lot of exposure created by Dennis," Spurs guard Vinny Del Negro said. "But he did his work on the court. And despite all the things that were said and all the things that were done, we were winning, and winning covers up a lot of things. When you lose, that's when they come to the forefront."

Inevitably, that's exactly what would happen.

For with everything else going on in his life, Rodman had a new distraction.

And this one was unbelievable.

thirteen
COPYCAT

"One thing I'll say is this: She taught him how to

get a rise out of the public."

Doc Rivers

adonna is onstage in Chicago, seated next to Oprah Winfrey, and the studio audience is buzzing at the presence of a living legend.

She is on a promotional tour for her new movie, *Evita*, and she is bubbling with the radiance of a new role—motherhood.

But it is basketball season in Chicago, and there are more pressing matters to discuss.

Like a certain ex-boyfriend who broke the code.

An ex-boyfriend who sold off the most private details of their relationship, a man no longer welcome in Madonna's circle of friends.

An ex-boyfriend that Madonna would just as soon forget.

> **Oprah:** I know that you surround yourself with people who care about you. Were there people who cared about you who said, "This is not a good idea"?
>
> **Madonna:** I think there were people who thought I had a momentary lapse of sanity. But that has happened before.
>
> **Oprah:** So you do what you want to do?
>
> **Madonna:** Look, I only dated him for two months. It's not like we were, you know, living together or engaged or something.

In April of 1994, Madonna was in a strange transition period. She had recorded just two albums in the previous seven years, neither of which were flying out of record stores. Her latest effort, *Erotica*, sold a mere two million copies, and its musical content was largely ignored, smothered by the thrusting sexuality of accompanying videos.

She had left behind a trail of bad movies, and after her meteoric ascension, there was much clamoring that her career had finally burned out.

She was also making headlines for her menu of male friends, forging relationships with baseball slugger Jose Canseco, hockey star Mark Messier, and a relatively unknown basketball player named Brian Shaw, a member of the Orlando Magic.

And she soon developed a crush on Dennis Rodman.

Jonathan Van Meter, then editor in chief of *Vibe* magazine, remembers picking up a newspaper and highlighting a telling quote.

"She said that Dennis Rodman was the Madonna of basketball," Van Meter said.

At the time, Van Meter was collaborating with Madonna's publicist, Liz Rosenberg, on an upcoming interview with *Vibe*. Madonna was willing to work with the magazine, but with one stipulation: she wanted to do something different, something out of the ordinary.

As soon as Van Meter read Madonna's quote about Rodman, he picked up the phone.

"Madonna and basketball players had been the hot topic," Van Meter said. "Dennis wasn't a big star yet, but he was sort of punk. He wasn't hip-hop, he liked rock 'n' roll. He didn't fit into the mold when you thought about black culture.

"I called Liz and asked if Madonna would be willing to do a Q-and-A with Dennis. She called right back and said yes, and I mean, she called back *instantly*."

After weeks of coordination, all parties arranged to meet at Madonna's house in Miami. Rosenberg, in fact, volunteered to catch a plane and pick up Rodman in person.

"Liz was that afraid that he wasn't going to show up," Van Meter said. "I guess he was notorious for that."

But once he did, the fireworks began.

"It was a matter/antimatter explosion," Van Meter said. "The second they were together, you just knew something bizarre was going to happen. They were all over each other right away. It was blatantly sexual from the start. They're both overtly sexual, flirtatious people, and not afraid to show their bodies.

"In fact, Dennis was on the front lawn changing his clothes in front of everybody. I mean, *I* saw him completely naked."

After a lengthy photo shoot of the two in various intimate poses. Van Meter handed Madonna a tape recorder. They disappeared to the front lawn, where Madonna conducted a two-hour interview.

Van Meter's original plan was not extensive. The feature was to include a page of photographs and a scant five hundred words of text. The title of the article was Madonna's idea: "Game Recognizes Game."

For some unknown reason, the story never ran in *Vibe*, a piece struck down by a high-ranking editor. Van Meter never understood the decision, and resigned his post shortly thereafter.

But for Rodman and Madonna, the sparks kept flying. Rodman stayed at Madonna's house the night of their interview, embarking on a furious, high-energy relationship that defied description.

Madonna cared much about Rodman, and did her part to make the relationship work, even flying to Utah to be with Rodman during the playoffs. And while she denies some of Rodman's outrageous claims regarding their sex life and her desire to bear his child, Madonna was, by all accounts, smitten with her new boyfriend.

Bryne Rich, Rodman's friend from Oklahoma, was around during much of their courtship. And he verifies Rodman's claims that Madonna was deeply infatuated with the NBA star.

"When Dennis first told me that Madonna wanted to go out with him, he really couldn't believe it himself," Rich said. "But she really liked him a lot. I saw some of the letters that she would fax him, and you should see some of the stuff she was saying."

Such as?

"Well, you can just imagine," he said. "Some of the stuff she was saying was crazy.

"She was looking for a relationship, and once they started going out, Dennis really started digging her. But you know Dennis . . . he can't stay with one girl."

The relationship clearly had strange and lingering effects on Rodman. In his autobiography, he bounces back and forth between two perspectives, still saddled with much confusion.

He was, no doubt, in awe of the relationship and its implications. For most of his adolescence, he was shunned by girls, embarrassed by his own appearance. Suddenly, he became rich and famous, and less than a year after breaking his anonymous mold in Detroit, he landed an international sex object.

Now he was waking up with Madonna, a notion he had scoffed at on Roy Firestone's television show just a month before. At the time, the attraction was incomprehensible to Rodman, who had no idea what he could offer a celebrity of her magnitude.

And yet to suppress the anxiety and insecurity of dating a pop icon, he reacted with aloofness. In his book, he devotes twenty-five pages to their courtship, sparing no details about their sexual tendencies and reacting to various nocturnal requests with strange detachment.

Although the relationship was brief, it was intense, and on the brink of becoming a serious venture. And there can be no arguing that Madonna served as a turning point in the evolution of Dennis Rodman.

She is a self-made superstar with remarkable courage and strength in the area of self-expression and redefining her own identity. She has an undeniable fearlessness that allowed her to break traditional boundaries. She had the uncanny ability to constantly change her look, to stay one step ahead of the game.

After entrancing pop culture with the oozing sexuality of a boy toy, she began challenging the very notion of femininity, chopping her hair and toning her body to the po obsession. She traded in the chips of blatant sexuality for the liberation of raw power, and began using uninhibited nudity not to attract men, but to display her own independence and character.

She pushed the limits of social acceptance with videos from *Erotica* and a voyeurish movie entitled *Truth or Dare*, in which she unabashedly displayed an appetite for bisexuality and sadomasochism. And she bared all, fantasies included, in an ill-fated photobook, simply titled *Sex*.

She expanded her audience, becoming a heroine to the gay community. She was a leading advocate in the battle against AIDS. She flaunted her shifting sexuality, which now included a few female friends. Yet behind the curtain, there was the constant undercurrent of a shrewd strategist, a woman who knew exactly how to tweak the public and become rich in the process.

Rodman would watch, learn, and copy every facet of the Madonna shock-value phenomenon.

Even if he won't admit it.

"No, because I was doing all of this before I met Madonna," Rodman said. "Nobody really realized that I was doing all of this. When I got with Madonna, people said, 'You did this because of Madonna, you were with Madonna, you learned a lot of tricks from Madonna.'

"You learn a trick or two, but as far as entertaining or marketing, you cannot get that [from somebody else]. You have to be creative and crafty enough in your own mind that you can go and do this. How many famous people do you know that can market themselves? Not many. Not many."

In her interview with Oprah Winfrey, Madonna did not seem angry with Rodman. Rather, she seemed genuinely hurt, burned by a man whose innocence belies his appearance.

In a diary published in *Vanity Fair*, Madonna describes how she reacted to Rodman's book:

"Woke up this morning feeling like a truck had run over me. My insomnia has resurfaced the last few nights and I'm trying to figure out why. Is it because a certain disgusting basketball player I made the mistake of going out with decided to publish an autobiography and devoted a whole chapter to what it was like to have sex with me? Complete with made-up dialogue that even a bad porno writer would not take credit for. It's so silly, I'm sure no one will take it seriously, but I don't feel like reading the headlines, and of course I feel exploited once again by someone I trusted and let into my life."

Madonna, no doubt, feels somewhat responsible for the rise of Dennis Rodman. And she should.

After their relationship ended, Rodman became one of the first athletes to publicly champion the fight against the HIV-virus, incorporating the symbolic AIDS ribbon into his hair color.

He began challenging the notion of masculinity through cross-dressing. He posed on the cover of *Sports Illustrated* attired in leather and a dog-collar necklace, conjuring up the same sadomasochism images that Madonna had popularized.

And he began to openly talk about a new journey to the core of his sexual being, about his slowly emerging fantasies of sleeping with a man, his growing desire to be bisexual.

If it is all an act, and it probably is, he owes Madonna for the lessons in self-marketing. Instead, he tramples on her in his autobiography, making her part of the process.

And this is why she feels used.

Doc Rivers, who came to the San Antonio Spurs in Rodman's second season with the organization, remembers sitting on a plane and listening to Rodman talk about his former flame.

"He admitted that he learned everything from Madonna," Rivers said. "He said, 'She's the best thing that ever happened to me in that aspect. Not only did she tell me things, but I watched her do it. I learned from the best. Just being around her . . . she's a genius.'

"So Dennis did the same thing with a basketball that Madonna did with a microphone, and he's done it well."

To that end, Rodman learned to yank the two most reliable strings of public reaction. He claims to have pondered suicide, peering into the chasm of death, ready to seal his own mortality.

"Madonna taught Dennis how to get a rise out of the public. She taught him everything he knows."

Doc Rivers

That, by his own admission, is fiction.

And now he's pulling the chain of conventional morality, voicing his growing fascination with bisexuality. And just like Madonna, his apparent honesty made him a beacon of light in the gay community.

By cross-dressing, painting his nails and wearing makeup, he has wandered into forbidden ground in the testosterone-driven world of professional athletics. And for the courage of his conviction, he was championed for remaining true to himself and not buckling under the mores of society.

And where would this register on the polygraph machine?

Is this too a blatantly transparent act?

There is a growing notion within the gay community that Rodman is simply using the stance of bisexuality as yet another form of self-promotion. After all, talk is easy.

In an issue of *The Advocate*, a national gay and lesbian news magazine, Rodman is adroitly interviewed by a writer named Peter Galvin in the gymnasium of a New York hotel. And depending on your perspective, Rodman either comes off as lost in the changing winds of his own sexuality or incriminates his own credibility with a few suspect answers.

One part of the interview is centered around Rodman's experimentation with kissing a transvestite.

Q: When you kiss a man, do you get aroused? Have you ever gotten an erection?

A: Not really, because I wasn't really putting myself in that position to have sex with them.

Q: So you were just toying with these guys?

A: No. I mean if I toyed with them, I think they'd realize what's going on. I was being affectionate . . . but with transsexuals, guys that have implants but still have big penises.

Q: You made out with transsexuals?

A: Oh, yeah, yeah. One.

Q: Did you get an erection?

A: Oh, of course.

"They're worried why I'm going around saying I'm gay. At least I'm bold enough and man enough to come out and say, 'Hey, yeah, I've thought about it, and one day maybe it'll happen. One day it will happen.' "

Dennis Rodman in *The Advocate*

Q: Why?

A: Because it's walking a fine line between a man and a

woman. If you talk to friends of mine, they'll tell you that I have made out with this one transsexual. Fuck, I mean so beautiful as a man and as a woman! I admit it. The motherfucker is beautiful. He has tits. They're like this [indicates breasts], and he looks like Marilyn Monroe, totally, totally. Hell, yes. I mean, if he didn't have a—

Q: If he didn't have what, a dick? Does that turn you on more than just being with a woman?

A: Well, I'm in between. I'm splitting the difference between a man and a woman. He looks like a woman, has curves like a woman, but he's a male. That doesn't frighten me because there's the security factor that this guy looks like a woman.

Q: You just said that doesn't frighten you. So does that mean that having sex with a man frightens you?

A: No, because like I said—

Q: Dennis, are you sure?

A: Totally, it doesn't frighten me at all. But I got to make sure that *that's* what I want. I just can't fuckin' jump in just because he's sexy.

Rodman also gives a glimpse of his intentions when asked what prompted his notorious book-signing appearance in 1996, when he showed up at a New York bookstore in a wedding dress.

"I wanted to fulfill something that one man couldn't do," Rodman said. "Not many men would wear a wedding dress down Fifth Avenue in New York, knowing you'd get a lot of bad criticism, a lot of bad flak, people calling you psycho, gay, bastard, and homosexual, things like that.

"I took the chance. It was fun. It was exciting. It was different. I'm not going to just go to a book signing and just walk in—Hi, how are you doing? I've got to do something that's entertaining for people, so people say, 'Well, shit, wasn't that a great day? Remember that day?'"

So, clearly, it's more about expanding his image than the liberation of his own sexuality. And some of Rodman's closest friends say that, despite appearances, Rodman is as heterosexual as they come. A ladies' man in every sense of the word.

But one thing is certain: from the day Madonna walked into Rodman's life, it would never be the same.

He no longer called himself a basketball player.

He now viewed himself as an entertainer.

"She was out in Salt Lake City with the team. She had a big limo, she'd come by and her and Dennis would take off together. It was pretty strange."

Bob Bass, former Spurs general manager

The relationship may have opened Rodman's mind, sharpening his own knack for how to garner attention, but it couldn't have come at a worse time for the San Antonio Spurs.

They opened the playoffs with big dreams, and they were only enhanced after blowing out the Utah Jazz, 106–89, to begin the postseason.

But late in Game 1, there were hints of trouble. Rodman became entangled with Utah's Bryon Russell, prompting Lucas to grab him from behind. Rodman spun around angrily, as if he were about to slug whoever had grabbed him.

In Game 2, Rodman exploded in a 96–84 loss to the Jazz. He undercut Utah's Tom Chambers under the basket, drawing a technical foul. Later in the game, he blatantly stuck his knee out to stop

John Stockton, injuring the Jazz guard and earning another technical foul. He was ejected from the game and began swearing at the Utah bench as he walked off the court. The NBA predictably reacted, forced to make a statement.

The league fined Rodman $10,000 for the incident, another $250 for the ejection, and suspended him without pay for Game 3.

Rodman's relationship with Madonna had been a laughable novelty among his teammates. But now, as they'd watch Rodman disappear into her limousine after the games, they were wondering whether he was pumping up the volume to impress his famous girlfriend.

With Rodman serving his suspension, the Spurs couldn't compete with the Jazz in Game 3, losing 105–72. Rodman promised to "go to war" in Game 4, and with Madonna seated courtside, he repeatedly tangled with Jazz players, earning another technical foul to accompany his 20 rebounds.

But the Spurs were done. They lost 95–90, and a promising season had ended in the first round of the playoffs. The Spurs' demise was more about David Robinson's disappearing act than about Rodman's uncontrollable nature—but both played a part.

"Maybe that [Madonna] thing was a mistake, maybe we could've controlled it better," Bass said. "If Dennis was with us [mentally], I don't think we would've had a problem. All we needed was for him to be there."

One gets the distinct feeling that Rodman wishes he had controlled the Madonna thing a little better, too. She has obviously moved past the strange chapter in her personal life, but has Rodman?

In his recent interview with Barbara Walters, he apologized for writing a chapter about his sexual relationship with Madonna.

In hyping his show on MTV, he keeps longing for an interview with Madonna, saying it would break all pay-per-view records. And in a brief Q&A with *Entertainment Weekly*, there is this passage:

Q: Are you going to get Madonna's baby a present?

A: Of course.

Q: What will it be?

A: If it's a boy, I'll get him a Dennis Rodman jersey.

Q: But it's a girl.

A: I'll still get her a Dennis Rodman jersey.

Back onstage in Chicago, Winfrey continues her conversation with Madonna:

Oprah: He said you wanted his baby.

Madonna: Really?

Oprah: That's what he said.

Madonna: *(long pause)* Well. Hmmm. He's lying.

Oprah: He's lying?

Madonna: I only dated him for two months.

Oprah: Have you seen him or talked to him since he betrayed you?

Madonna: No.

Oprah: And it was betrayal?

Madonna: Absolutely. Yes.

Oprah: And I would think with all that has been written and said about it, that whatever you all had, at least you probably thought you had a friend who wouldn't betray you.

Madonna: I thought he was my friend, yes.

Oprah: And you feel now you could never be friends because he says now that he'd really like to apologize.

Madonna: Really?

Oprah: Yeah, I read that.

Madonna: Well, he better crawl from here to China.

fourteen

"I know people don't understand me, and I like it that way. I like it when people can't figure me out and don't know what to expect. But they should never be afraid of something or somebody different. Life is full of the unexpected."

Dennis Rodman

Although the San Antonio Spurs had finished one victory shy of a franchise record, the fallout from the postseason flop was significant.

Bob Bass, the team's operations chief, was quickly fired. John Lucas, the head coach, was called before an executive committee of eight owners and told that they were not pleased with how much freedom he had given Rodman. Lucas saw plenty of trouble ahead and submitted his resignation.

And in an unusual move, the Spurs' managerial team of twenty-two owners voted president Bob Coleman out of office, turning over the reins to Gregg Popovich.

"They wanted to make sweeping changes," Bass said. "But to say [Lucas] didn't have control of the team was wrong. To say that the team was in disarray was wrong. And to blame Dennis for everything that happened just wasn't right."

The turnover marked a significant change in leadership, a sign that the club was going to demand more discipline and structure for the upcoming season.

But to Rodman, the implications were far greater.

With the drastic changes in the Spurs' hierarchy, the principals who had promised a hefty raise for Rodman were gone. And so was the proposed one-year contract extension for $6 million.

Before the start of the 1994–95 season, the new management tried to convince Rodman and his agent that they would take care of their power forward in the future. But they were not bound to discussions they had no part of, and would not honor what they deemed "nonbinding conversations" with the previous regime.

Rodman was incensed. Still soured by the upheaval in Detroit, his view of business in the NBA became irreparably skewed. And as much as the Spurs tried to move ahead, reacquiring Sean Elliott from the Pistons and hiring Orlando Magic assistant Bob Hill as new head coach, Rodman was no longer on board.

Rodman showed up a day late for training camp, missing a team meeting and a practice session. He then blew off an exhibition game against the Milwaukee Bucks, and was fined $15,000.

"He was scarred. He felt he was lied to. He felt used. A lot of guys feel that way, but Dennis took it to another level."

Bob Hill, former San Antonio Spurs coach

When he finally reported to camp, Hill knew he had problems.

"He was scarred," Hill said. "A lot of players are lied to and used, and the same is true for coaches. It's a very contradictory existence. Some deal with it professionally, some don't. NBA basketball is all involuntary cooperation; players think, 'I have a talent. Pay me what I deserve, or you won't have my talent.'

"Dennis decided to exercise his involuntary cooperation. But I had a different picture of Dennis than anyone else in the organization. I tried to beat his ass for four years [as head coach of the Indiana Pacers], and I couldn't do it. I grew a great respect for what he could do on the basketball court."

Before Rodman's first exhibition game in Mexico City, Hill tried to smooth the rough edges. He went into the locker room, where Rodman was riding a stationary bicycle, simultaneously watching game tape on a nearby television.

He tried to empathize with Rodman's plight.

"I said, 'Look, for whatever it's worth, I believe everything you said. I believe there was a promise, and you deserve to be paid what your market value is. I'll do everything I can to help you get there,' " Hill said.

"Maybe I shouldn't have said anything because I don't think he trusted me at that time."

He trusted nobody, and the surly behavior continued throughout training camp. And after Rodman was ejected from the team's final exhibition game for cursing officials and throwing an ice bag at Hill, the Spurs acted aggressively. He was suspended without pay for the first three games of the season.

Rodman again felt disrespected, unappreciated, and unfairly persecuted for last season's playoff disaster. He didn't have his extension, and before playing a regular-season game, he had already lost $90,000 of his $2.4 million salary.

And yet he was determined not to lose this battle. He was now a rebel, and his newfound individuality had caused his popularity to soar. He would be a martyr, if necessary, but there would be no turning back.

A day after his three-game suspension was scheduled to end, Rodman again missed the next two practices. Rodman was called to a special meeting with Popovich, and after thirty minutes of bickering, there was no resolution to the growing problem. Rodman agreed to take an indefinite leave of absence, although the Spurs would pay him during his hiatus.

Popovich originally thought the leave of absence would last ten days. It stretched into three and a half weeks, and the Spurs struggled out of the gate, compiling a 7–8 record. They were expecting Rodman to return with a revamped attitude on December 7, having undergone team-mandated psychological counseling with his personal psychiatrist in Detroit. But when practice convened, all they got was a phone call.

It was Rodman, who said he was in Dallas. He claimed the keys to a friend's truck were stolen from his pocket, and that some of his possessions were also heisted. The team changed his status to suspended without pay, and while the Spurs were losing another game to the Utah Jazz, Rodman was spotted working out on a StairMaster at an upscale health club in San Antonio.

The next day, Hill received another phone call.

It was Rodman's agents—he now had two of them—and they were conveying a strange message.

"I was told that Dennis didn't want to play anymore," Hill said. "I said, 'That's ridiculous. I have to talk to him. I told him to meet me at the practice site, and we'd talk. If he didn't want to play after our meeting, then fine, don't play.' "

Rodman showed up for the meeting, but without any equipment. And yet he was remarkably calm, and surprised Hill with his perspective. He agreed to attend a practice, borrowed a pair of shoes, and joined his teammates on the floor.

"I just knew he had to get through one practice," Hill said. "We knew that, unless his psychologist was on the take, they had met every day [during his leave of absence]. The players knew this, too, and it was an embarrassment to Dennis. But after we got through one practice, he was fine."

Hill was determined to build a solid foundation of teamwork, and had Rodman meet with the three team captains—David Robinson, Avery Johnson, and Terry Cummings. After the meeting, his teammates were convinced, and Rodman was reinstated.

So on December 12, Rodman finally played his first game of the season, contributing five rebounds and six points in a 122–101 rout of the Washington Bullets. But his statistics didn't matter nearly as much as his presence.

When he entered the game late in the first quarter, he received a standing ovation from the San Antonio crowd. And his arrival, combined with the acquisition of free-agent point guard Glenn "Doc" Rivers two weeks later, immediately pumped life into a staggering team.

"I came to San Antonio because of Dennis," Rivers said. "I remember at a press conference, I said I had picked San Antonio because they were the team that had the best chance of winning a championship, and people thought I was a freakin' nut."

Rivers, in fact, had spurned offers from eight other teams, accepting the least amount of money being offered—a league-minimum $150,000 from the Spurs.

"They were under .500 at the time, but I knew with a backup point guard, they would have an incredible bench," Rivers said. "And since Dennis had returned to the team, I thought they had a great chance of winning a championship."

Rodman, as usual, simply resumed his role as if he hadn't missed a day of practice in his life. Rivers gave the team a greater sense of stability and maturity, and the Spurs featured the kind of depth rarely seen in the NBA.

Hill's starting lineup featured Robinson, Rodman, Sean Elliott, Avery Johnson, and Vinny Del Negro; his bench consisted of J. R. Reid, Cummings, Rivers, Moses Malone, Willie Anderson, and Chuck Person. This team was significantly stronger than last year's unit that won 55 games in the regular season, and with Rodman, Rivers, and Malone, it had a good measure of playoff experience.

As soon as Rodman returned, the Spurs embarked on an incredible streak of dominance. After missing the first 17 games of the season, Rodman's sparked the team to a 17–5 record over their next 22 games.

The contrasting records surely exaggerated Rodman's role, but the fans ate it up. A new ritual had begun with some of Rodman's hardcore fans, who began showing up at the Alamodome with their hair dyed green, matching the color of their favorite player's scalp.

When he switched colors from green to orange to purple, so did the fans. And a separate row began wearing metallic green wigs in honor of Rodman.

"I don't have the star status of Michael Jordan, but I have the other side of Michael Jordan," Rodman said. "I can relate to the kids, pretty much because I am a kid, playing a man's game. But I have a great time doing it. The kids love coming out to see Dennis Rodman, with his colored hair, his tattoos, and this and that. I like to shock people. I like to give them something different to look at and maybe cheer for."

And they did, mainly because Rodman was once again a remarkable force inside for the Spurs. He tipped in a rebound with eight seconds left to lead the Spurs to a 97–96 victory over the Sacramento Kings; he had 20 rebounds in a victory against the Lakers;

in a rematch against the Kings, he had 22 rebounds and broke a tie by sinking the decisive free throw with 35 seconds left, guiding the Spurs to another one-point victory; and he pulled down 27 rebounds in a victory over the Seattle SuperSonics.

"Dennis had problems with certain things. But winning covers up everything."
Vinny Del Negro, San Antonio Spurs guard

The Spurs were on fire, largely due to Rodman. His inside play allowed Robinson and Elliott to roam the perimeter, where they both felt more comfortable. And Rodman continued his personal tear.

He had 30 rebounds in a victory over the Houston Rockets, a season-high in the NBA; he had 21 rebounds in three quarters of play against the Cleveland Cavaliers; and he scored off an offensive rebound with three seconds left, leading the Spurs to a one-point victory over Orlando.

It was now March 10, and the Spurs were in the midst of an amazing run. They were 18–2 in their last 20 games, and 33–7 since Rodman returned to the lineup on December 10.

But all the while, Hill knew this was an uneasy truce.

"I was concerned about his frame of mind," Hill said. "The psychologist said that [Rodman's behavior] could go in and out at any time, and you just don't know when it was going to happen.

"If John Lucas was coming back to town, it had an effect on him. If his mother or Alexis or any other family member were coming to the game, Dennis would always know exactly where they were sitting. And if they weren't in their seats, Dennis wasn't worth a damn until they got there. There's a side to him that really cares about people, more than anyone ever realizes. And his way of getting back at people is a little bit different."

Sure enough, during the zenith of the Spurs' ascension, when everything was going so well, Lucas, now coaching the Philadelphia 76ers, arrived in San Antonio for a game at the Alamodome. And when the Spurs gathered in the locker room before the game, Rodman was AWOL. He showed up in the second quarter, but never emerged from the dressing room.

"If his mind is on basketball, it's a sharp mind, very intense, very good for the people around him," Spurs guard Avery Johnson said. "If it's not, well . . ."

Rodman told team officials that he was victimized by the strangest of circumstances, that he had overslept because his alarm clock failed to go off. He claimed an electrician contracted to rewire his house had left the electricity off, disabling the alarm clock. He said the electrician realized the mistake while listening to the Spurs' game on his car radio, panicked by reports that Rodman hadn't shown up for the game. He turned around, sped back to Rodman's house, and woke up the power forward.

Publicly, team officials accepted Rodman's excuse and declined any further punishment.

Privately, they knew better.

For whatever reasons, Lucas's presence in San Antonio rekindled all of Rodman's furor over the broken promise.

"I got there in mid-season, but the damage had already been done in Dennis's mind," Rivers said. "He felt he was done wrong by the organization, and he couldn't get past it. The new management had promised to take care of Dennis after the season, but he had heard that before, and there was no trust. That's when the fiasco started."

And even though the Spurs were wildly successful, Rodman carried a certain disdain for some of his teammates. He didn't like the softness or makeup of the team, and never tried to hide his dissatisfaction with David Robinson, a perennial All-Star.

"He was not a David Robinson fan," Rivers said. "He didn't think he played hard enough. He didn't think [Robinson] competed, or had any heart. One of the first things he told me was, 'Doc, you're a warrior. We need [Robinson] to be more like you. Our main guy ain't got no heart.'

"Hearing that, you knew there were problems. But he believed it."

Rodman also objected to some of Hill's rotation patterns. With such a deep bench, Hill had designated a "New York" unit, which was comprised of his best scorers. This unit was used in specific stretches when the Spurs needed to score.

Rodman balked at the notion, saying no one could provide his kind of offensive rebounding. This was true. But along with those rebounds, Hill realized the risk of Rodman being fouled and sent to the free-throw line. And that's not what any coach wanted at the end of the close game.

"I remember this one game against Cleveland, I called for the New York unit, and we diagrammed a play in the huddle," Hill said. "I wasn't paying any attention to Dennis, but we all knew the play was going to work. As soon as Sean Elliott made the shot, I started running into the tunnel, pumping my fist.

"I was really concerned with his frame of mind. A psychologist said he can go in and out at any time. You just don't know when."

Bob Hill

"I look up, and Dennis is running *out of the tunnel,* and he's also pumping his fist. I stopped, and realized just what had happened. Dennis had left the court and watched the end of the game on television in the locker room. I just bent over, and started laughing my ass off. The guy is priceless."

Yet this was serious, and the Spurs' coaching staff knew exactly what was going on inside of Rodman. They worried about his lapse against the Philadelphia 76ers, and hoped his absence was just a fluke, not a portent of things to come.

But they were in no mood to take chances, and following a staff meeting after a Saturday night game, assistant coach Dave Cowens had an idea.

Cowens shared Rodman's affinity for motorcycles, and had been invited by Rodman to join him and a few friends on a motorcycle trip the following day. Cowens thought it might be a good idea, thinking he could bond with the disenchanted player and exercise some damage control before things got out of hand.

Gregg Popovich was all for it, convinced Cowens could talk some sense into Rodman. Hill was not so agreeable, leery of the consequences.

"I said, 'You can't do that during the season, it's written in all NBA contracts [that players can't ride motorcycles during the season],' " Hill said. "And to send a coach with him? I had been in so many meetings with Dennis, and I knew it wasn't going to work. I knew it wouldn't have any impact."

Hill's wishes were ignored, and he spent the next afternoon at a movie. When he returned, there were two messages on his answering machine. One said that Dennis Rodman was in the hospital, and Hill jumped in his car, knowing his worst fears had become reality.

That afternoon—a gorgeous spring Sunday in San Antonio—Rodman was surprised by a stop sign. He slammed on the brakes and went tumbling off the bike. He separated his right shoulder, and would be out for two to four weeks.

At the hospital, Rodman was accompanied by Jack Haley and his two agents. The doctor had just finished his examination, and Rodman was struggling to put on a T-shirt. As soon as Hill walked into the room he was cornered by the agents, who requested an on-the-spot meeting. They found a vacant room in the hospital and began to talk.

"They were scared we were going to suspend him for the rest of the season for breaching his contract," Hill said. "They were trying to get Dennis to apologize to me, but Dennis wouldn't respond. He was pissed off, hurting, looking the other way."

Finally, Rodman decided to speak, and he let loose.

"Let me tell you something," Rodman began. "They've got seventeen games left. If those motherfuckers can't win seventy percent of the games for the rest of the season, then fuck them motherfuckers. I got them to where they are now. If they can't go the rest of the way, fuck 'em."

Hill calmly turned to the agents.

"See, that's what his attitude is like all the time with this team," Hill said. "I don't know why you're trying to get him to apologize to me."

Hill stood up and left the room. All the while, he knew the Spurs couldn't suspend Rodman for breaching his contract, since the team had in effect not only condoned the motorcycle excursion, but sent an assistant coach along for the ride.

The following day, Hill walked into practice. He gathered the team in the locker room and wrote the number 17 on the board. He told his players that the number signified how many games they must overcome in Rodman's absence, and symbolized how many additional rebounds they must collect to fill the void.

The Spurs were 44–18 at the time, and on the heels of a 35–9 stretch, were in the running for the top seed in the Western Conference.

Instead of falling apart, they bought into Hill's approach. Cummings and Reid picked up the slack, combining to average 16.8 rebounds per game over the next three weeks, just under Rodman's average. They went 12–0 without Rodman, extending the team winning streak to 15 games. They passed Utah for the Midwest Division lead, and were on their way to home-court advantage throughout the Western Conference playoffs.

All the while, Rodman brooded. He had apologized to the fans and the team for his motorcycle accident, but felt indifferent about the Spurs' spectacular winning streak.

"Every time we won a game without Dennis, it hurt him," Hill said. "He really believed he was the one who made us go.

"Dennis wasn't with us for most of the time, and I wasn't paying a hell of a lot of attention. I knew Dennis, in his own way, would fight us if we tried to help. But I also knew he was tremendously proud of his body, and he would get himself ready to play. I wasn't worried if he was flying to Las Vegas, because I knew when the time came, he'd be ready."

Near the end of his rehabilitation, team officials wanted to get Rodman back with the program. They insisted he travel with the team, and while Rodman belligerently fought the notion, he accompanied the Spurs on a trip to Sacramento.

Rodman's demeanor had worsened during his absence, and at one point, Popovich threatened to suspend and fine Rodman for not signing basketballs with the rest of his team as part of a community relations project.

During their stop in Sacramento, where his ex-wife and daughter live, Rodman visited Alexis. And after another massive fight with his ex-wife—the screaming matches were almost legendary among Rodman's friends—he was a human tornado. He complained bitterly about having to accompany the team when he couldn't play, and tore into Cowens during a special meeting.

Rodman walked out of the conversation, caught a plane, and went home.

"Dennis obviously had some problems with certain things," Del

Negro said. "There were some differences, and for the most part, Dennis did what he had to do, and the organization did what they felt they had to do. But once he was on the court, there was no denying how hard he worked."

After missing fourteen games, Rodman finally returned to the lineup on March 15, and received a twenty-five-second standing ovation when he entered the game.

The Spurs rode out the string, finishing with a franchise-best 62–20 record, the best in the NBA. Although he played in only 49 games, Rodman returned in time to surpass the necessary 800-rebound minimum, winning his fourth consecutive rebounding title with a 16.8 average.

The Spurs brushed off the Denver Nuggets in the first round of the playoffs, and Rodman was spectacular, scoring 19 points and grabbing 16 rebounds in Game 2 of a three-game sweep.

The Spurs' chances were also buoyed by the Lakers' stunning upset of the Seattle SuperSonics. They would host the Lakers in the first two games of the conference semifinals, and for the first time in ages, a small southwestern town had visions of the impossible: winning an NBA championship.

"The guys were so close they could taste it," Hill said.

"Dennis just didn't like the team, and he hated David Robinson. He told me all along what was going to happen under pressure because he thought they were a collection of pussies."

Bob Hill

The Spurs opened the Western Conference Semifinals with a pair of victories on their home court. Yet both games were surprisingly tough, and the Spurs seemed apprehensive and out of synch, needing overtime to prevail in Game 2.

In Game 3 at the Forum in Los Angeles, the Lakers were energized by their own fans. And after L.A. built a 10-point lead late in the game, Hill called time-out.

Rodman had already been removed from the game and had taken

off his shoes, wrapped a towel around his head, and was lying down on the floor.

The players gathered around Hill, but Rodman remained motionless.

"C'mon, Dennis, let's go," Hill barked.

No response.

After giving instructions to his players, Hill took a few steps toward Rodman.

"Don't even think you're putting me back in the fuckin' game," Rodman said.

"Don't fuckin' worry about it," Hill said.

Just like that, chaos enveloped the San Antonio Spurs, and their mission was in extreme jeopardy.

The next morning, Hill walked into the locker room, and immediately called a team meeting. Rodman was sitting inside one of the huge stalls in the visitors' locker room, wearing sunglasses, staring at the floor.

Hill began ripping into Rodman, telling him that he was immature and selfish, that he had put his own agenda in front of the team.

"I told him, 'You're not playing tomorrow; I don't give a fuck if we lose by a hundred points, you're sitting on the fucking bench,' " Hill recalled.

With Reid and Cummings combining for 21 points, the Spurs toppled the Lakers 80–71 in Game 4. Rodman chatted with a fan during the game and smiled for the cameras, but he never took his shoes off, and he participated in the huddles.

The Spurs returned to San Antonio for a chance to earn their first Western Conference Finals berth in twelve years. Rodman didn't start, but came off the bench to contribute 11 points and 15 rebounds.

But the Lakers wouldn't go away, and forced overtime when Nick Van Exel netted a three-pointer with 10 seconds left.

The Spurs held a 96–95 lead in the closing seconds of overtime, but the Lakers had the ball and were working for the final shot. Elden Campbell missed a finger-roll with four seconds left, but the rebound slipped out of Rodman's reach. The ball ended up in the hands of Van Exel, who drained another three-pointer with under a second left, and the Lakers prevailed.

On the flight back to Los Angeles, Hill sensed impending disaster. He took a seat next to Avery Johnson, and devised a plan.

"Do you want to win tomorrow?" Hill asked.

Johnson looked at his coach like he was an idiot.

"Well, if you do what I tell you, we'll win tomorrow," Hill said.

"Okay, what do you got?" Johnson said.

"You have to go up to Dennis and Jack [Haley], break the ice, maybe play some video golf with them," Hill explained. "Just bullshit with them a little bit. Just go up there and make it seem like you're reaching out to Dennis. Then when we get to the hotel, go to his room, and let him tell you how we can beat the Lakers.

"Maybe he'll make some sense, maybe he won't. But he'll feel like you came to him, that you need him."

Johnson again flashed a disbelieving glance at his coach.

"Okay, I'll do it," Johnson said.

When the plane landed, Hill patted his point guard on the behind. "Good luck," Hill said.

The next morning, Hill was having breakfast in the hotel lounge by himself. At 7:15, Johnson marched triumphantly into the restaurant, taking a seat next to his coach.

"Coach, you wouldn't believe it," Johnson said. "It worked. I even told Dennis to go tell Sean [Elliott] what he had to do to stop [Cedric] Ceballos. He bought into the whole thing."

Rodman responded in a big way. Back in the starting lineup, he had 12 points and 16 rebounds. Johnson was superb in running the show, dishing out 11 assists and scoring 13 points. Robinson dominated in the paint, posting 31 points and 15 rebounds. And the Spurs throttled the Lakers 100–88, advancing to the Western Conference Finals against the Houston Rockets.

"Dennis had his best game of the entire playoffs, he was just phenomenal," Hill said. "The problem with doing what I did is that I couldn't do it again. I had played my trump card. But I really felt we could beat Houston, and certainly, seeing an opportunity to make it to the [NBA] Finals, he wasn't going to do anything disruptive now."

Hill pauses.

"Well," he says. "I was fuckin' wrong."

After Hill gave his team a day off, the Spurs were to attend a team dinner the next day where they'd prep for the upcoming series. It would be an informal affair, where they'd pass out books on the opposition, discuss travel plans, and watch tape. But it was mandatory.

That morning, Hill was talking to a friend when his other line beeped.

He switched over, and heard the voice of Haley.

"The saga continues," Haley said.

"What's up?" Hill asked.

"He's in Vegas, and he won't come back until you call him."

As it turned out, Rodman was being interviewed for a *Sports Illustrated* cover story. After their clinching victory over the Lakers, Rodman, Haley, and the entourage were going to show the scribe just how rebellious he is. On a whim, they boarded a flight for Las Vegas, and after much revelry, Rodman decided he didn't want to attend the meeting.

Hill placed a call to Rodman, who answered immediately.

"Dennis, how the fuck you doin'?" Hill asked. "Winning any money?"

"Fuck no," Rodman said.

"Well, we're got a meeting tonight," Hill said.

"Why do we have to have a fuckin' meeting? That's bullshit," Rodman said.

"That's fine, but we're having a meeting, and you have to be there," Hill politely insisted. "Winning any fuckin' money?"

"If I didn't have to come to the fuckin' meeting I'd make some money," Rodman said.

"Okay, see you at the meeting," Hill said.

Rodman returned, but the Spurs lost Game 1 on their own court. Robinson scored just 21 points, his lowest production of the postseason, and Elliott missed two free throws and a shot in the lane in the final 25 seconds.

While Rodman grabbed 20 rebounds, he removed himself from the huddle on numerous occasions. And when the Spurs took the floor with a chance to win the game on their final possession, Rodman was not on the court. The New York unit was, and Rodman took off his shoes in disgust.

The next day, *Sports Illustrated* hit the market. Rodman was on the cover, holding his macaw, wearing a leather outfit and a rhinestone dog collar around his neck. The article detailed Rodman's excursion to Las Vegas, and how he wanted to blow off the team meeting and show up for Game 7 of the Rockets–Phoenix Suns series. It also served as the first public disclosure of Rodman's alleged bisexual fantasies, and how he visualizes "being with another man." He claimed not to "give a —— about basketball anymore," and posed provocatively in his transvestite garb.

The story did not go over well in some corners of San Antonio. Just hours after publication, an unknown person with a bottle of shoe polish scribbled "FAG" on Rodman's pink and white truck. The next night, when the vehicle was parked outside a gay bar, another person slashed the tires.

But it didn't have the same effect on his teammates. In fact, it did quite the opposite.

"We had a fun time with that," Doc Rivers said. "Dennis walked into practice the next day and even he was laughing about it. It got him to laugh with the team, and that was a rarity. He rarely talked to anyone, and in a strange way, it sort of brought us all closer together."

After practice, the gags continued. Moses Malone was sitting alone at his locker, about to take a shower, when Rodman walked into the room. Malone jumped on the opportunity:

"Woman in the locker room! Woman in the locker room! Everybody grab their towels and cover up!" Malone screamed.

As the players howled with laughter, Rodman couldn't contain his grin. He too began laughing.

"We had a great time with that," Rivers said. "See, the guys couldn't care less about his sexual orientation . . . whatever it was."

But the humor quickly disappeared. In Game 2, Hakeem Olajuwon lit up Robinson, scoring 41 points in the Rockets' 106–96 victory. They had won the first two games at the Alamodome, and held a commanding 2–0 advantage in the series.

Rodman spent a curious twenty-one minutes on the bench in Game 2, and sat alone on the Spurs' bench long after the final buzzer had sounded. He was not a factor, finishing with four points and eight rebounds, and would later say he was hurt by the lack of playing time. Hill claims there was no hidden reason for his diminished role, that strategy and matchups had dictated his substitution patterns.

The series moved to Houston, and the Rockets could close it out with two wins at home. But, inexplicably, the series would swing like a pendulum. The Spurs prevailed in Game 3, pulling out a 107–

102 victory. And Rodman came alive in Game 4, dominating the Rockets in an emotional performance. He scored 12 points, and 12 of his 19 rebounds came on the offensive end.

The series was now tied, and moving two hundred miles back up

the interstate to San Antonio. But the momentum was clearly in the Spurs' corner. They had clawed back into the series, and were giddy with accomplishment.

Less than twenty-four hours later, there would be another crisis. And this would be the last.

"The Spurs had a real shot at winning a championship, but Dennis just wasn't happy."

Doc Rivers

Hill had scheduled a workout for the following day, and as the team assembled on the floor, Rodman was nowhere to be found. Ten minutes after practice was supposed to start, Hill told his players that if Rodman didn't show up soon, he wouldn't be starting Game 5.

There was silence on the floor.

They knew the importance of the moment, aware they were on the brink of one of the most important games in franchise history. They knew they couldn't win without Rodman, and yet they couldn't believe he'd let them down now. They hemmed and hawed, subtly pleading with Hill to refrain from taking a hard stance.

"All at once, they could see the Finals, they could see the rings on their fingers," Hill said. "Their attitude was changing."

Rodman did show up, but he was forty-five minutes late. He told the trainer he was suffering from a mild bout with the flu, but many of his teammates and coaching staff suspected he was hung over.

With the national media waiting for interviews, they kept Rodman in the trainer's room.

When pressed on the matter, Hill told reporters that Rodman had a "stuffy nose." When asked if he was in the building, Hill told the media that Rodman was in the back lifting weights.

"You can lift weights with a stuffy nose," Hill said with a certain sarcasm.

When finished, Rodman ducked out the back door. And later that day, Hill received a phone call from Popovich, who wasn't so sure about the plans not to start Rodman in Game 5.

"He asked if we were cutting off our nose to spite our face," Hill said. "I couldn't believe what I was hearing. I told Pop, 'We defined ourselves this way all season long and now we're going to buckle under pressure?'

"He said, 'Well, we need him.' I said, 'I know we need him, but this is about building teamwork. Anytime we get close, he tests us. This is nothing new.' "

Finally, Hill and Popovich devised another plan. Hill would call Avery Johnson, who would canvass a few key players. If they decided Rodman should start, he would. If they concurred with the coach, he wouldn't.

Johnson reported back to Hill, saying the only person he could find was Rivers. According to Hill, Johnson said that Rivers had agreed with taking the consistent approach.

"We decided that the whole season was about tolerating distractions on a day-to-day basis," Hill said. "Why should we change now? If we were going to let him get away with that kind of stuff, we should've let him do it from the very beginning."

So Rodman watched the opening tip-off from the bench, and although he entered the game at the 4:49 mark of the first quarter, the damage had been done.

Olajuwon was once again unstoppable, burning Robinson for 42 points. Rodman finished with just 5 points and 12 rebounds, the Spurs committed 22 turnovers, and the Rockets waltzed to a 111–90 victory.

Inside of the Spurs' locker room, Rodman went ballistic. He began beating the walls, crying, screaming obscenities at Hill and Popovich. Hill tried to ignore Rodman, delivered a brief message, and walked out of the room.

The Spurs were toast. They flew to Houston, and their season once again ended with indignity. The lost 100–95 in Game 6, and a team on the brink of destiny was in complete shambles.

"Dennis was terribly irresponsible," Rivers said. "Coach Hill made a decision not to start him. They felt they had to make a statement, and that statement cost us the playoffs. And that statement was not their fault.

"Some of the players were for it, some were against it. I didn't know which way to go. I just felt I was being punished for something that I didn't do. Was it the right decision? In ways, no, it was not. We should've fined him, taken his money, and put him on the court. And then you play his ass forty-eight minutes, make him die out there on the court. Because this was my shot at winning a championship, and by punishing him, they were punishing all of us.

"But Dennis forced them into that decision. He told me, 'Hey, Doc, honestly, I overslept.' But Dennis was the one who was late, the one who didn't feel it was important enough to wake up. If I make a mistake or David Robinson makes a mistake, that's one thing. But if you've done it fifteen times . . .

"At some point you have to make a stand, but in Game Five, he quit because he was pissed off about not starting. In Game Six, he was awful, didn't do a damn thing for us. As much as I like him as a basketball player, I lost a lot of respect for him during the Houston series."

There was no chance of reconciling now. Near the end of Game 6, Rodman put the wrecking ball to his career in San Antonio.

Robinson was struggling late in the game, and on two consecutive possessions, he missed a pair of easy shots close to the basket. On the third possession he was fouled.

When Robinson missed the first free throw, Rodman walked away from the lane, looked at Hill, and threw his hands up in disgust.

"They call me a baby and they call me selfish, but I bust my ass on the court. I do the dirty work, yet they say I'm not a team player. I do a lot of things other players won't do."

Dennis Rodman

When Robinson missed the second free throw, Rodman ran downcourt, glancing at Hill on the way. This time, he was shaking his head.

"Like he was saying, 'I told you so,' " Hill said.

The season had begun with Rodman missing the team bus to the opening day of training camp. It ended with Rodman blowing off the team charter to San Antonio after a season-ending loss.

Once again, there was a pathological symmetry, a circular madness to Rodman's slash-and-burn existence.

"He's the most selfish individual you'll ever run into," said one member of the Spurs' hierarchy. "Everything is for Dennis. Talk to him about his daughter, and he'll cry for you. Turn the camera on, and he'll act for you.

"It didn't work here in San Antonio for two reasons: it wasn't the last year of his contract, and he didn't believe in David, so he separated himself. Nobody blamed him for the playoff loss to Houston, but he just said that because he thought it would bring him sympathy. He's what all of us would fight against with our children. Everything he does is from a narcissistic standpoint.

"But all of that said, we still wouldn't have gotten rid of him except he made it clear he didn't want to be here any longer."

When Rodman forced the Pistons into a corner, they reacted badly, brought to their knees by his unending antics. Billy McKinney traded him to the Spurs for Sean Elliott, who arrived in Detroit with talents depleted by a kidney ailment. The following season, McKinney traded Elliot back to the Spurs for a player named Bill Curley. It was a botched series of trades from which McKinney would never recover, ultimately losing his job.

Now the Spurs were in the corner, and couldn't wait to unload Rodman. Problem was, every team in the league knew of the Spurs' desperation, and the franchise would be scorched one final time by Rodman's involuntary cooperation.

"All I have to say about Dennis is the season began with him missing the bus to Kerrville and ended with him missing the plane to San Antonio. You fill in the blanks."

Bob Hill

As for Hill, well, he would last another full season before getting fired—and replaced—by Popovich just two months into the 1996–97 season, on the eve of David Robinson's long-awaited return from an injury.

And believe it or not, Hill has never wavered in his fondness for Dennis Rodman.

"I like Dennis a lot," Hill said. "There's just something about him . . . Because after all is said and done, he did it his way. And there's a part of me that wants to say, 'God bless you. You pissed off a lot of people, you hurt some people along the way,' and he scares both coaches every time he steps on the court.

"But he stays loyal to himself. He is what he is. If you like it, he doesn't care. If you don't like it, he doesn't care. And there's a part of me that respects that."

sixteen
PROMISED LAND

> "I think they thought I'd come in, be a distraction, turn this team into a circus and destroy the organization. Well, great minds overcome all."
>
> **Dennis Rodman**

ennis Rodman hovered over a microphone, staring at two thousand people who had gathered for the Chicago Bulls' annual tip-off luncheon in the Hyatt Regency ballroom.

As he began to speak, a silence came over the room.

"Playing with Michael Jordan, Scottie Pippen, and the Chicago Bulls doesn't mean anything to me," Rodman said. "That's just the way it is."

Blasphemy.

A sure sign that the anti-Christ had come to town.

But instead of throwing forks at the stage, the crowd began cheering.

And it lasted for sixty seconds.

In the midst of the roaring signs of approval, one fan screamed over the crowd:

"We love you Dennis!"

Three seats away, Michael Jordan couldn't help but grin, shaking his head in disbelief.

Rodman continued.

"But I do respect these guys. I've got to hand it to the Bulls. They really had a great team those three years they won. I want to come here and give 110 percent. If I don't do that, I need to get the hell out of here. But I'm going to do that."

Again the crowd burst with enthusiasm, and Rodman walked away from the microphone, returning to his seat.

"I understand they're a little leery, a little cautious having someone like me in here. They wonder how I'm going to respond to the team."

Dennis Rodman

On October 2, 1995, the Bulls took a gamble that turned the basketball world on its ear. They traded Will Perdue, a competent yet stiff reserve center, to the San Antonio Spurs, and plucked away Dennis Rodman and his suitcase full of problems.

Talent for talent, this was a steal, and everyone knew it. Of course, there was also a well-documented downside that followed Rodman like a curse. But Bulls owner Jerry Reinsdorf happened to be in the mood for a little game of high-risk, high-reward, and happened to think he had the right people to control Dennis

Rodman. One was Phil Jackson, whose mastery at dealing with people and problems set him far above any coach in the NBA, including Pat Riley. The other was Michael Jordan, whose indomitable presence would, in itself, do much toward keeping Rodman in line.

Besides, the previous season was an ink-stained indignity to the legacy of a team that was now two years removed from its string of three consecutive championships. Jordan had staged his stunning return to basketball at the end of the previous season, but was painfully awkward in the playoffs, particularly down the stretch of close games. The Orlando Magic overcame fourth-quarter deficits to win three of the four games in their series victory, and when it was over, Horace Grant was hoisted on the shoulders of his teammates, waving a white towel to the United Center crowd.

Now *that* was blasphemy.

Grant had bolted the Bulls the previous season via free agency. Reinsdorf claimed afterward the two had reached a verbal agreement on a new deal, only to have Grant break his promise. Either way, there was much animosity between the two sides, and Grant's victorious return left a sour, indelible mark on the organization.

In the Bulls' decline, the Houston Rockets had forged back-to-back titles, and had an opportunity to match the Bulls' three-peat. The very notion of the Rockets reaching the same stratosphere was ludicrous, and it was time to make a statement.

The Bulls were initially interested in Jayson Williams, but he wanted too much money. General manager Jerry Krause turned in the direction of Dennis Rodman, and Reinsdorf was immediately intrigued. He gave his blessing if Krause could pull it off.

Given his age, experience, and the fact that he had a year remaining on his contract in San Antonio, Rodman also had certain leverage over his new address, and could veto any proposed trade.

He wanted out of the Spurs organization as badly as Popovich did, but he also desired a warm-weather climate—like, say, Los Angeles. Dwight Manley, Rodman's new agent, had a better idea.

Manley and Rodman had been friends for nearly four years, having met at a craps table in Las Vegas. As the friendship grew, Manley, who had made a fortune in coin collecting, became concerned with Rodman's finances. He had offered to take over the role of agent, and devised a plan to get Rodman solvent again.

Fact is, his careless lifestyle and affinity for gambling had left Rodman broke. He had nothing left of the $2.5 million he earned with the Spurs, and not a penny in the bank from his previous earnings. In a profile by *Smart Money* magazine, Rodman disclosed that he had no cash to cover a $9,000 monthly alimony payment to his ex-wife; a $3,800 payment on his Ferrari was past due; and the $500,000 dollars he borrowed for the purchase of a home had remained unpaid for five years, and with interest, the debt had grown to nearly $750,000. Add it all up, and Rodman was more than $1 million in debt.

But Manley knew that people loved winners, and in Chicago, the soil was rich and fertile. Rodman consented. And while he was leery of how he'd be received in a city that once despised his every move, Rodman flew to Chicago for a weekend of interviews, meeting with Reinsdorf, Krause, and Jackson.

"Dennis has had some psychological damage in his maturation process," Jackson said. "He reminded me of a kid sitting in the back of the room, wearing his headphones and listening to music when the teacher is explaining a theory in the classroom. And while he appears not to be paying attention, he is very focused on everything that's going on.

"Normal conversation are very difficult for Dennis, and eye contact is impossible. But I don't think there had ever been a situation where people have sat down with Dennis and talked to him about what they want. We just made the effort to see where he was at and whether we could communicate.

"We made an agreement that he would come here with a clean slate. We were going to ignore what had gone on before; whatever problems he had in the past would stay in the past. We were going to abide by the rules laid down by the team, and he would have no exclusivity.

"We knew that he had been disappointed in the past, that promises had been made and not fulfilled. Whatever had gone on, he couldn't have those same expectations. But there were a few things we thought we could do that would be beneficial to him."

For instance, Jackson was sympathetic to Rodman's financial plight. And he made a promise that, if given enough notice, he would extend Rodman the freedom to capitalize on certain opportunities.

"We told him if he had, say, a guest appearance in Oakland for $100,000, and he gave me ample notice, we would give him the time off," Jackson said. "Or we'd let him miss a weekend practice to help him get back on his feet."

Rodman trusted Jackson, Jackson trusted Rodman, and they all thought the relationship could work where all others had failed. After the interview process had ended, Krause wanted to close the deal, and called Jackson at home.

He had promised his coach the luxury of final approval, and while Jackson was stoked by the challenge, he told Krause he needed clearance from his team captains.

Jordan, who was burning with the challenge of regaining his throne, agreed without much hesitation. But Jackson knew Pippen would be a harder sell.

"I talked to Scottie specifically about having a personal vendetta," Jackson said. "I asked if it would affect his ability to play together.

"He said, 'No. I don't see myself dealing with Dennis off the court. I'm not going to extend myself to be his friend. But as long as he wants to come on the court and prove he is a teammate, then I have no problem.' "

Just like that, the transaction was complete.

"Dennis ought to say a prayer to Gregg Popovich every day when he wakes up for sending him to Chicago," said Dave Cowens. "Pretty nice of him, huh?"

Indeed, but no one could have anticipated the kind of fervor the acquisition would unleash. To basketball fans in Chicago, Rodman had been the symbol of all evil. But the moment he became a member of the Bulls, the city went absolutely mad, delirious that such a mercenary menace would now be fighting their battle.

They extended a group hug to Rodman as if they were throwing their arms around a troubled child, soothing his demons with kindness and filling his ears with unconditional support.

It was a kinetic reaction that went beyond explanation. It was a city with a rich history of heroes, from Dick Butkus to Walter Payton, Ernie Banks to Bobby Hull, Gale Sayers to Frank Thomas, and of course, Michael Jordan. It was a city that revered its blue-collar athletes, guys who succeeded with limited talent and unparalleled courage. In that regard, Rodman upheld the civic image fortified by guys like Mike Ditka, Jerry Sloan, Carlton Fisk, and Mike Singletary. Yet Rodman also tapped into the city's fondness for the unpredictable, following the wild tradition of Jim McMahon, whose wackiness was incredibly tame by Rodman's standards.

It was a powerful combination of identities, and despite his rap sheet, Rodman returned to the scene of the crime as an instant fan favorite.

"After they sealed the trade, I walked into Jerry Krause's office and we high-fived each other," said Steve Schanwald, the Bull's vice president of marketing. "Chicago has always loved lunch-bucket guys, and we knew he would appeal to the adults. But they also fell in love with his colorful personality, and to kids, he was almost like a cartoon superhero come to life. And on top of it all, he was an archenemy, an archvillain who came to a team and became a beloved hero. It was amazing."

And beyond. Entrepreneurs couldn't market Rodman hard enough to meet the demand, and when a giant mural of Rodman was painted on a building that overlooks the Kennedy Expressway, it caused traffic jams and a pattern of accidents involving people who slowed down to stare at his likeness. The mural lasted a week before city officials demanded that it be erased.

"It's amazing how there can be a 180-degree turnaround," Jordan said.

More than anything, the fans were consumed with the possibilities of dominance, the delicious prospect of regaining a championship team. In Las Vegas, the Orlando Magic were posted as 4–1 favorites to repeat as Eastern Conference champions. After the signing of Rodman, the Bulls were moved up to 5–1.

The tone was set early. The Bulls won their first three preseason games by an average of nearly 20 points, Jordan was in preretirement form, and the excitement in Chicago was already at a fever pitch.

"I have no fear. Not one man or two men can stop Dennis Rodman. Only Dennis Rodman can stop Dennis Rodman."

Dennis Rodman

"Almost immediately in the exhibition season, we could see Dennis's effect on the crowd," Jackson said. "We thought we would have to do more of a selling job among the people in Chicago because he went against the image of what we considered a Bull-type personality.''

All the while, Rodman soaked in the glow of his new appreciation. And for the first time in four years, he seemed genuinely happy with his teammates.

"We're mean here," Rodman said in the preseason. "In San Antonio, we had guys who liked to go home and be breast-fed by their wives. You've got guys here who are ready to rock and roll every damn night."

"On paper," said Jordan, "this could be our best team ever."

Late in the preseason, Rodman endeared himself to the crowd after diving into the stands for a loose ball. But he came up limping, and after starting the first three games of the season, was sent to the injured list with a calf strain—the same injury he had in Detroit leading up to his alleged suicide attempt.

He missed the first twelve games of the season, but with Jordan burning up the league, the Bulls bolted from the gate.

When Rodman returned, the Bulls were simply phenomenal. The trio of Jordan, Pippen, and Rodman gave the Bulls what was arguably the best off guard/small forward/power forward combination in the history of the league.

In 1996, Dennis Rodman was voted a first-team, All-NBA defensive player along with Scottie Pippen and Michael Jordan. It marked the first time in history that three players from the same team were selected.

Rodman provided the rebounding the Bulls had sorely lacked the previous season. His one-on-one defense in the paint made the Bulls the stingiest team in the league. And his energy instilled a throbbing pulse on a team already brimming with determination.

But it was a strange mix of professional camaraderie and social isolation. Rodman would ride on the front of the team bus, speaking to no one while his teammates played cards in the back. He again had Jack Haley as a confidant, signed by the Bulls as a third-string center. But in a city that cherished his abilities, the role of loner was getting wearisome.

So on a road trip in January, Rodman extended himself. After the Bulls had beaten the Philadelphia 76ers at the Spectrum, Rodman told his teammates he would be at a bar downtown, and they were welcome to join him.

Rodman left, and the rest of his teammates devised a plan. They would pretend to blow off Rodman's invitation, only to show up just before closing time. And that's exactly what they did, shocking Rodman just as they had hoped. It was a gesture that broke massive chips off the iceberg, and the entire team headed off to an all-night bar.

The next day, after flying to Washington, D.C., they reported to practice. Jackson knew precisely what had happened.

"I could tell some of them were dragging," Jackson said. "I told them they all smelled like they had slept in a brewery or woken up in the gutter. Fortunately for them, there was a leak in the roof, and we shortened practice."

Jackson, however, was in the mood to cut his team some slack. He wanted Rodman to feel more in tune with his teammates, and a group hangover was a small price to pay.

"From that point on," Jackson said. "There was inclusion of Dennis inside the group."

The Bulls were now on pace to win 70 games in the regular season, a feat no team had accomplished before. According to Jackson, the team had reached a "heart space" with Rodman, who had been ejected from only one game. His behavior had been exemplary, his play a marvel of consistency.

And then came inevitable disaster.

In late March, the Bulls were playing the New Jersey Nets in a meaningless game when Rodman was beaten to the basket on a driving layup by Armon Gilliam. Rodman slammed the ball to the ground in disgust, and was given a technical foul.

He was then whistled for a loose-ball foul on former teammate Rick Mahorn, and while pleading his case, he stuck his hands down his shorts. Ted Bernhardt, another referee standing fifteen feet away, called a second technical on Rodman.

And Rodman lost his mind.

He ran over to Bernhardt, and during a heated discussion, delivered an infamous head-butt to Bernhardt's forehead.

He was pulled away by teammates, but Rodman's rage was just getting started. He knocked over a water cooler, stripped off his jersey, and before leaving the court, he began gesturing wildly and shouting obscenities at the officials.

And it all happened with Rod Thorn, the NBA's vice president of operations, in attendance.

Coincidence?

Rodman was nailed with a six-game suspension, and fined $20,000. His lost salary amounted to $207,000, and once again, he had fallen off the horse.

"Physical assaults on referees cannot and will not be tolerated," Thorn said. "I just can't allow that. If I did, there would be anarchy."

It was the ninth suspension in Rodman's career, and just like all the others, it seemed incomprehensible to the culprit.

"Rod Thorn is sitting ten feet from me, and when I get kicked out, I get a phone call not even five minutes after the game from NBA security," Rodman said. "And he's in Milwaukee [while] Rod

Thorn is standing right besides me. He said, 'What did you do?' I said, 'Well, I didn't do anything.'

"I was talking [to the other referee], and I put my hands in my pants, saying, 'Do you want me to guard him like this?' Then the other guy thinks I'm telling him [to perform an obscene act], and he throws me out.

"I head-butted him . . . suspend me, make an example out of Dennis Rodman. I don't care. It's getting ridiculous, picking on me every damn game."

This time, Rodman would soon recognize the implications. Jordan, Jackson, and Pippen were extremely disappointed in Rodman, and great concern arose in Chicago about whether or not he endangered the masterpiece in progress. Rodman sensed all of this, knowing he had messed up the ideal situation.

"At the time, I felt he could go either way on us," Jordan said. "Someone had to reach out to him and bring him back into focus."

That was Jackson, who conducted an individual meeting with Rodman. And later that night, Rodman called Jordan in his hotel room, asking if he had an extra cigar. Jordan was stunned.

"I began to see how disappointed he was in himself, on how what he was doing could be a harm to the team," Jordan said. "He's never called me on the road, and we've never talked at a hotel. But at that time, I think it was his way of saying, 'Hey, I'm sorry.' "

Once again, Rodman's absence didn't hurt the Bulls. Jackson inserted Toni Kukoc into the starting lineup, and in the six games Rodman missed, the Bulls won five, with Kukoc averaging 17.7 points, 6.2 rebounds, and 5.4 assists per game. All told, Rodman would miss 18 games due to injury or suspension, and the Bulls went 15–3.

When Rodman returned, the Bulls were 62–8, well on pace for the NBA record of 69–13, held by the 1971–72 Los Angeles Lakers.

But Jackson kept Kukoc in the starting lineup, bringing Rodman in off the bench.

TOP REBOUNDING PERFORMANCES AT AGE 34

Bill Russell	19.3
Wilt Chamberlain	18.2
Dennis Rodman	14.9
Wes Unseld	13.3
Elvin Hayes	11.1

The Bulls would win 10 of their last 12 games, bounding into the history books with a 72–10 record. Rodman won his fifth consecutive rebounding title (14.9 per game), and though he had lost his starting job, he never said a word, and was the model of proper conduct.

"I felt like I had let the team and the fans down," Rodman said. "I mean, everything was going along so smooth and I was being a good boy and all. The Bulls were treating me good, and so was the whole city of Chicago, and then along comes something like this."

He would get his redemption in spades.

After a first-round sweep of the Miami Heat in the playoffs, Rodman rejoined the starting lineup in a best-of-seven series against the New York Knicks, and worked his postseason magic.

He was constantly baited by the physical Knicks, but never came close to losing his composure. He concentrated on becoming part of the offense for the first time in the season, surprising the Knicks with his scoring. And in a decisive Game 5, Rodman reached double digits in scoring for the first time, scoring 11 points and grabbing 12 rebounds. The Bulls disposed of the Knicks on Rodman's birthday, and were poised for a showdown with the Magic. And to celebrate, Rodman left the United Center with Pearl Jam singer Eddie Vedder and bassist Jeff Ament to his own birthday bash at a Chicago nightclub.

The party, however, was just getting started.

As it turned out, the Magic were no match for the Bulls. Grant would be injured in the first game of the series and never return. And as much as Shaquille O'Neal tried to carry the Magic, he couldn't solve his nemesis.

The Bulls throttled the Magic 121–83 in Game 1 at the United Center, and in the second half, Rodman held O'Neal to one basket over a stretch of 7:31. It was a foreshadowing moment, and O'Neal would never overcome his frustration with an undersized forward who illustrated his defensive brilliance.

After Game 1, O'Neal called Rodman a "gimmick," and Rodman just smiled.

"I am a gimmick," Rodman said. "And if he thinks I'm a gimmick, that's great. He's going to be a great player . . . someday. I do my job when the time is right, and I do what it takes to win. That's why people love the person that is Dennis."

"I said to him right before the playoffs, 'Don't you love this?' He said, 'You know, this is what it's all about.'"

John Salley, former NBA player

And after the Bulls rallied from a large deficit to capture Game 2, O'Neal was asked what he now thought of Rodman.

"Nothing . . . never," O'Neal whispered.

Obviously, O'Neal was done, smothered by Rodman's defense and a prisoner of psychological warfare. The series moved to Orlando, but the outcome was inevitable.

"Caught in the act: emotions of a janitor turned thief."
(Courtesy of the Dallas–Fort Worth Airport Department of Public Safety)

"Big fish in a small pond."
(Courtesy of Harold Harmon)

"Ancient history: looking normal and looking to score." *(Tom Smart /Allsport)*

"Nearing the end in Detroit."
(Tom Smart /Allsport)

"New team, new look,
new attitude."
(Allsport)

"Doing what he does best: rebounding and mugging for the camera."
(Nathaniel S. Butler/Allsport)

"Arriving in Seattle for the 1996 NBA Finals, and as usual, the first player off the bus." *(Jonathan Daniel/Allsport)*

"The missing link in Chicago and champion once again." *(Jonathan Daniel/Allsport)*

"Lacing up the shoes for another run with the Bulls." *(Jonathan Daniel /Allsport)*

"Drawing a crowd and starting a controversy in Utah." *(Todd Warshaw/Allsport)*

"Enjoying a cigar and another championship with Pearl Jam's Eddie Vedder." *(Courtesy of Matt Kryger/Copley News Service)*

Speaking to the masses at the 1997 Grant Park celebration: "I'll be back, baby!"
(Jonathan Daniel/Allsport)

In Game 3, the Bulls spanked the Magic 86–67, and O'Neal was so frustrated that, at one point, he threw Rodman to the floor.

"His game is totally off," Rodman said. "He was frustrated, but there was nothing he could do. That team is very young. They have a long way to go. This is our year. Heart can take you far, and if you don't have it, you don't have a chance.

"Their focus is not there, you can see it in their eyes. They didn't want to compete. They're like a cheap battery. They're going to last for a couple of hours, and then they're dead."

While the Magic sulked in their locker room, Rodman emerged from the locker room wearing a black bandana. He hopped in a limousine with "The Nasty Boys," a tag-team duo of professional wrestlers.

Rodman was on top of the world. His value had never been more evident, and his agitation never more effective. The Bulls swept the series the following day, but not before O'Neal received a technical foul for shoving Rodman to the floor, and not before Magic coach Brian Hill vented his anger by sniping at Rodman.

"Like they say, it was David and Goliath," Rodman said. "The bigger they are, the harder they fall. I hate to use a terrible cliché, but I won't let any man make me scared of who he is or what he does. I think Shaq realized that he was up against someone with a lot of heart, with a lot of desire and determination, someone who wasn't going to let anyone knock him on his ass. Not me."

As for Brian Hill?

"Brian Hill talks all that smack," Rodman said. "He can have a piece of me if he wants. Brian Hill is small in height and small in the pants."

Just like that, the Bulls were back in the NBA Finals.

The Seattle SuperSonics seemed to have the athleticism necessary to combat the Bulls in the Finals, but they immediately embarked on a strange strategy.

They used Frank Brickowski, a muscular enforcer-type, to try to get Rodman to implode, and the tactic backfired. Brickowski was ejected from Game 1 after throwing Rodman to the ground, and although Rodman was relatively quiet, the Bulls raced to a 107–90 victory.

When Brickowski walked off the court after his ejection, he engaged in an animated chat with the Bulls' bench, calling Jack Haley a "baby-sitter" to his face.

"People don't realize that Dennis does a lot of things to make people not realize what he's doing. A lot of it is distractions. A lot of it is him. But the fact that he has different-colored hair, the tattoos, the way he talks to the referees, the way he bumps guys and all that, he lets them think about everything else except what they're supposed to be doing."

John Salley

"We saw that coming a mile away," Haley said. "As soon as [Brickowski] came into the game, I told Dennis that he was going to get physical with him. It was pretty obvious what the intent was, but Dennis is a lot wiser and more professional than people think."

After the game, Sonics coach George Karl furthered the feud, saying Rodman deserved "no credibility" as a basketball player.

In Game 2, Rodman responded with 20 rebounds, and tied an NBA Finals record with 11 offensive rebounds, a mark set by Elvin Hayes in 1979.

In Game 3, the Bulls punished the Sonics 108–86 in Seattle, and were on the brink of a series sweep. The Sonics had clearly lost their way, sucked into the Rodman vacuum. Brickowski was once again ejected after elbowing Rodman in the throat and waving off a referee, and the Sonics were coming apart at the seams.

Rodman was beaming with his display of self-control, and the effect it had on the opposition. He called himself the "master of psychological warfare" and no one was about to argue. He even went so far as to deliver a little message to Karl near the end of Game 3.

"I know you're a great coach," Rodman said. "But you've got to teach your guys to play basketball again. Teach them that, instead of making it a one-on-one confrontation with Dennis Rodman."

Said Rodman: "It's all a mind game. If you get caught up in what I'm doing, you're screwed. I know how to play both sides, and I'm going to win that battle."

While the Sonics rallied to win their final two games at home, the Bulls clinched the title with an 87–75 victory in Game 6. Rodman was unstoppable in the series finale, grabbing 19 rebounds, and for the second time in the series, tying the NBA record with 11 offensive rebounds.

Michael Jordan was named MVP of the NBA Finals.

It could easily have been an award given to Rodman.

"I give him a lot of credit," Jordan said. "He came in with a lot of heart, and the rebounding he's done made the difference. Not just in the Finals, but throughout the playoffs.

"My attitude toward him has changed considerably. I became more forgiving and understanding as the season went on. Scottie is more hardened than I am because of the stitches he received, but at some point in the season, he started to give more respect to Dennis.

"I don't think he was trouble. I think he's smart. And I think he's very loyal to this team, and would do anything to improve our situation, to help us win. Whatever trouble he had coming into this season, he showed he can also be just as focused, and part of a situation."

Indeed, Rodman was wrapped up in a blanket of total vindication. When the championship had been sealed, he hugged Phil Jackson and jumped on top of Jordan, who was lying on the floor with the basketball.

In the hallway after the game, he worked his way through a mob of well-wishers, including ESPN's Dan Patrick.

"He wanted to kiss," Patrick said with a wry smile. "I wouldn't let him."

When Rodman finally stopped against a back wall, he delivered a speech he had been preparing all season.

"I don't think there was ever an instance when I thought he was going to cost us the opportunity to get back to the Finals."
Michael Jordan

"This is one of the biggest things to ever happen to me," Rodman said. "I survived all the critics, all the backstabbers, all the two-faced people who say I'm out for myself. Those are the people who just don't understand Dennis Rodman.

"I'm a team player. I was a team player all season, except when it came to my hair color and my clothes. The last four years have been hell for me, but I made it through. There are a lot of things about me that people don't realize, but the one thing they can't take away from me is that I'm a competitor, a fighter, and I go out there and work my ass off every night.

"I promised one thing to this city, and tonight, I delivered. I think I give the game of basketball a great name."

At that moment, Eddie Vedder stepped toward Rodman, who broke through the mob of media. He and Vedder clinked champagne glasses and headed off for an endless night of celebration.

"Time to go get drunk as hell," Rodman said.

seventeen

APPLE TREE

"When I hear about him, I shake my head and laugh. Thank God I had the sense to leave this man."

Shirley Rodman

The drinks are always flowing in the seedy town of Angeles, an outpost in the Philippines that is as close to hell as you're going to find in modern civilization.

But in this armpit city of vagrants, prostitutes, and other misfits, a man without morals is enjoying a life of newfound fame.

After three decades of decadent exile, Philander Rodman resurfaced on the map of consciousness in the summer of 1996, beaming with pride over a son who helped lead the Bulls to the NBA championship.

The Bulls were an international story, and nearing the age of sixty, Philander Rodman had become a local celebrity of sorts. Television and newspaper reporters had flown from Manila to chronicle his life story, and upon hearing of his lifestyle, *The Washington Post* dispatched a reporter named Keith B. Richburg to find Rodman's notorious father.

He found Philander Rodman running a dingy bar called Full House, a dark tavern with a new legacy. The walls of the bar are adorned with a Dennis Rodman jersey, just like the one his father wears to work. There is also a Dennis Rodman poster, the *Sports Illustrated* cover that turned his image into a national conversation piece, and assorted newspaper clippings of his son's exploits.

Richburg also reported that Philander Rodman had sired twenty-seven children, and is shooting for thirty. He has two wives in the Philippines, who live in separate houses, and rationalizes the practice of polygamy by claiming to be a Muslim. Together, his two wives shelter fifteen of his children.

"They think Dennis bad," Rodman told *The Washington Post.* "They ain't been around me . . . They ain't seen nothin'. I'm the bad one."

Indeed, Philander Rodman makes no excuses for his behavior, including the day he left his wife and three kids over thirty years ago. He remarried just a week after divorcing Shirley Rodman, and his second marriage lasted seven years.

He claims to be a victim of a destructive cycle, repeating the same behavioral patterns he witnessed as a child. Philander told the *Post* that his own father deserted him when he was six years old, but they later reconciled once he understood his father's dilemma.

"I don't know him and he doesn't know me."

Philander Rodman, Dennis's father

"I used to hate my father," he said. "Later on, when I got married, Dennis' mother gave me such a . . . hard time; I understood it wasn't my daddy's fault."

Not only does Philander Rodman feel completely justified in his actions, but carries his cloak of adultery with an eerie sense of accomplishment.

"You want to change scenery every once in a while." he said. "You get tired of cake every day. You want pie!"

Despite his own exploits, Philander Rodman is now living vicariously through his first child, and is desperately trying to rekindle a relationship he left for dead many years ago.

He claims to write and fax letters to Dennis on a constant basis, but to date, has heard no reply.

"I understand Dennis' bitterness towards me," he told Richburg. "I don't ever plan to ask him for anything. I didn't make the money—that's his money. I just like to look at him and say, 'That's my son.' "

Philander Rodman then held up a copy of his son's racy autobiography.

"You can't control me. You can't control him," he said. "When I see him talk, I look at me. When I see him walk, I look at me. When I read this, I'm reading about myself.

"I think he'll understand one day. I hope so, anyway. I hope he'll come around."

"I hear him brag about having twenty-seven children, and I just laugh. Thank God it wasn't me."

Shirley Rodman

Shirley Rodman shudders when she hears about the inevitable comparisons between father and son. The man she first married is still floating through life, completely devoid of any moral center. His appetite for women has never waned, his distaste for commitment has never changed, and he stands for absolutely nothing.

Yet Philander Rodman delights in his son's outrageous exploits, convinced that they were spawned by his seed, and that he is thereby ultimately responsible. And when Dennis Rodman is championed by the masses, applauded for his individuality, it provides a scary confirmation of the life Philander Rodman has chosen.

When Dennis Rodman hears about his father, is he looking at his own future? Is he destined to complete the same cycle of empty existence? Or will the bitterness toward his father enable him to wade through the shallow waters of a life without meaning?

On the surface, it appears the apple hasn't fallen far from the tree. And in this case, the original fruit is rotten to the core.

It is a frightening prospect, a dark picture of what can happen to a man rambling through life without a road map.

"No, Dennis is not going to be like his father," Shirley Rodman insists. "All that talk about sex and romance and women being a dime a dozen, to Dennis, that's all for show.

"Dennis will eventually have to come to grips with himself. I know. I faced that myself."

eighteen

MOMMA'S HERE

"I am so proud of him, and so pleased that some people know he is for real as a person."

Shirley Rodman

With a new ring tucked away in a safety deposit box and a resuscitated career gaining steam, Dennis Rodman left Chicago with an ambitious agenda, wiping out any thoughts of a summer vacation.

But early in the off-season of 1996, he received a phone call from his mother.

"I asked him for ten to fifteen minutes because I don't get a lot of time with Dennis," she said. "We don't get to say private things.

You can't even have lunch or dinner with the child, and when you do, it's mostly in gay communities because they don't bother him.

"But I wanted to know where he was at [mentally] because he started doing so many things."

The sudden whirlwind of attention and her son's new status had left Shirley Rodman reeling. She still lived in her 1,100-square-foot apartment in Dallas, but her shroud of privacy had been pierced. Now she was the famous mother, and with a phone number listed in the public directory, she was easily accessible.

And she was beginning to get annoyed.

"When the Bulls won the championship, my life was hell." Shirley said. "All of a sudden, everyone wanted me on every show. I thought, 'What is going on?' It disrupted everything in my life."

Indeed, what happened in June 1996 was a revelation to Shirley Rodman, a glaring window to all her son had become. She was certainly aware of his persona, but not its magnitude. She is a quiet person who loves to read, far removed from the strange world that her son inhabits. And the less television she watched, the less she knew of her son's bizarre evolution.

"When he got to the NBA, he was in the fast lane, living life to the fullest. He just shut me out of his life."

Shirley Rodman

She had also felt "shut out" of her son's life for many years, their relationship fractured from Rodman's ties to the Rich family in Oklahoma, his time sapped by the demands and rewards of being a superstar. But all the while, she remained convinced that the values she instilled in Dennis were too deep-rooted to be smothered by his notoriety.

Her beliefs were reinforced when she accepted her son's offer to fly to Chicago and watch Game 1 of the NBA Finals in person.

But moments after stepping off the plane, she found more than she could handle.

Her son had become an enormous cross-culture celebrity, equipped with all the trimmings. He was unattainable, the epicenter of a seismic circle of friends. It was as if she dropped in on her son's life, opened the door, and found a wild party raging inside.

She didn't stay with Dennis at his modest home in the north suburbs, instead finding a room waiting for her at the downtown Hyatt. She was picked up at the hotel, taken to the United Center for the game, and seated next to a sweet, elderly lady.

It was Eddie Vedder's grandmother.

Vedder, singer and driving force behind Pearl Jam, had also come to Chicago for the first two games of the series, and accompanied his grandmother to the game. Long before tip-off, Dennis came over and introduced his guests.

Shirley apologized to Vedder for having never heard a Pearl Jam song in her life. Vedder smiled, insisting that it was nothing to worry about.

"He was such a nice, unassuming young man," Shirley said.

Yet it was becoming clear that Shirley Rodman was a silent tourist in her son's new life, and it was about to get worse.

When the game was over, Shirley thought she was embarking on a quiet dinner with her son. But when she got to the restaurant, she found Dennis in the midst of a huge entourage. She waited to be seated, but there were no open chairs left at the table.

"It was horrible," Shirley said. "Dennis had all these big-time people there. All the baggage was there. And Dennis was just looking at me."

The entourage scrambled to find a chair for Shirley, but it was too late. Her fierce pride had been wounded. She started crying, and rushed out of the restaurant. She hailed a cab, went back to the hotel, and cried some more.

In between sobs, the phone rang.

It was one of Dennis's friends.

"He asked me what was wrong," Shirley said. "I said, 'If you don't know what's wrong, then we really have a problem.' "

Click.

Finally, Dennis called the hotel. He was no longer aloof or indifferent, no longer the famous celebrity. The mask was gone, and he sounded like the son she once knew, properly concerned about the episode. He told his mother to calm down, that he would pick her up for lunch the next day.

He kept his promise.

"We went to this place that was almost falling down," Shirley said. "But we had two full hours together, and I was just thrilled to death. Those are the rare moments."

Shirley apologized for causing a scene at the restaurant. Dennis laughed off the whole incident. They would part amicably, and Shirley returned home, wondering when she would see her son again.

Over a month had passed before Shirley Rodman picked up the phone, requesting a visit from her son. And when Rodman opened a nightclub in Dallas, he obliged her wishes.

"I said, 'Dennis, where are we going with all this stuff?' " Shirley said.

"He said, 'Momma, I'm just making a living. If I'm going to go out, I'm going to go out with a big bang.'

"When we got past all of that, I asked him what he really wants to do. He told me he wants to come out of the NBA and not be broke. He wants to be able to give me things, and that really took my attention."

After much convincing, Shirley agreed to accept a token of her son's fame. He purchased a new home for his mother in a quiet

Dallas suburb, one large enough for Dennis to walk through without thumping his head on the ceiling.

It marked the end of a promise she had made thirty-two years ago—never to move again after returning home from New Jersey. And it symbolized a new beginning, one that will include an unlisted phone number.

There are times when she feels twinges of guilt, worried that she is somehow compromising a simple life of self-reliance, joining the long line of people who have benefited from her son's wealth. But she also knows her son's career is almost over, and maybe then he'll have more time to share. And maybe this new house that Dennis loves so much will make it even more enticing to drop by for prolonged visits.

For as she enters the autumn of life, Shirley Rodman desires only two things: a little peace of mind, and a little piece of the real Dennis.

"Dennis wants to give me the world," she says. "But I don't want the world. I just want Dennis.

"I would prefer not to have a famous person in my family. I like my little, passive life."

Her voice, soothing and sweet, develops an edge—the kind that must have surfaced on that horrible night in Chicago. And it is eerily similar to the temperament of her son, quiet and shy, softspoken and reserved, with a tolerance level that builds to a slow boil and then . . . all hell breaks loose.

"They managed to make me lose my identity for a while," she said. "I was 'Dennis Rodman's mom.'

"No, I'm not. I'm Shirley Rodman, and Dennis is my son. See, I never see the hair and the tattoos. I still see him as the young man that I raised. I look past all that stuff. I don't ask him about basketball, if he's taking all that other crap seriously. Because, eventually, I think it will all play out.

"As he weeds through the trash, all the people giving him wrong advice, he'll get back to what's real. Our relationship is durable, and it's going to last in spite of what everyone says.

"I think, when he's done with all of this stuff, he'll come back to me. He knows, deep down, who has been there for him."

When their chat was over and her son was ready to leave, Shirley escorted Dennis to the parking lot. In her quaint living room, she had rediscovered her son, if only for a few fleeting moments. But once they hit the pavement, people immediately started gawking, approaching her notorious child.

Just like that, memory lane had once again intersected with a painful present.

"Go away!" she screamed. "I want you people to get away from me! Get away from my son! Go away, he's not signing any autographs!"

Shirley Rodman begins laughing, embarrassed and yet amused by her own rage.

"I got so hateful," Shirley said. "That was my time, and I was ferocious. They were all looking at me like I was some preacher from Mars. All the while, Dennis was just laughing."

Yet Shirley didn't mind a bit, for it certainly wasn't the first time she had bared her teeth to protect—or motivate—her son.

Besides, it felt good, downright maternal. She was bonding with her son all over again in their fight against the world, reminiscent of a time when she was all he had.

She is longing to be needed once again, to be an active part of her son's life. In the past two years, she had sensed that the unspoken chill between her and Dennis had melted, that they were slowly bonding once again.

It is her hope for the future, the reward a long time coming.

"The last two years have been a joy in my life," Shirley said. "I think if you teach your children as well as you can, if you instill a center of beliefs in them, they will eventually get back to what is real. And I think Dennis will eventually come back to me."

nineteen
CURTAIN CALL

**"They know what kind of player Dennis is, and
what they were dealing with when he came to the
organization. You can't change Dennis."**

Scottie Pippen

 hen Dennis Rodman re-
turned for his second sea-
son with the Chicago Bulls, he was charting untested waters.

His status as an athlete had reached its zenith, and his dirty paws
stood out on the canvas of a sporting masterpiece, his indomitable
presence largely responsible for the greatest season in NBA history.
His defense and rebounding were so influential during the playoffs
that the Bulls were being hyped as Superman (Michael Jordan),
Batman (Scottie Pippen), and Rodman. He had come to a team with

two established superstars, and in one season, wiggled his way into equal billing.

That's unprecedented.

Stranger yet, he had come to town like a hitchhiker, in debt and holding a dark résumé. He was among the NBA's greatest character flaws, and his legacy clashed badly with his new address. For long before he left San Antonio in his wake, he was the most dreaded Piston of all, the man who made a hobby out of tormenting the Bulls, particuliarly Scottie Pippen.

Yet in one season, he had played into the hands of a compassionate city, pulling off one of the most stunning reversals in the history of public opinion. And under the constant threat of implosion, he kept his cool, and was once again in NBA champion.

He was a hero, like never before.

He had rekindled his wealth, gone Hollywood, and earned a shiny new contract with the Bulls for $9 million.

He fought his way back, stood on top of the mountain, and stuck out his tongue.

Okay.

Now what?

At thirty-five years of age, Rodman was again breaking new ground. He was seduced by his own reception, and kept pushing himself farther and farther near the edge. He gorged on attention, and the more he inhaled, the more he had to meet the need.

And he began to wonder:

Did he really need basketball?

Was he bigger than the Bulls?

The Bulls knew they were about to enter the dark alley on the map of Rodman's psyche. But they were the organization that salvaged his career, placed him in a high-reward situation, and didn't play games when it came down to contract negotiations.

Had the scenery around his core finally changed?

Or was it still as stale as it appeared in October 1996, when the Bulls gathered to christen a new season?

The hangover from last season was obvious and not confined to Rodman, for there was not enough time to decompress from the stratosphere the Bulls had inhabited for ten months.

For on June 16, the Bulls had capped the best season in NBA history with a championship. It was a season of breathtaking domination from the opening tip-off, a remarkable and exhausting run that included a 72-10 record, an 18-game winning streak, and an NBA-record 44 consecutive victories at home.

It was a tribute to a team that did the unthinkable, summoning the necessary focus for every game on their schedule. It was confirmation of Jordan's dogged determination and unparalleled greatness, an epic march in which he had recovered a throne he vacated while swinging at curveballs. And it was the bounty for a group that knew exactly how to coddle the inner mysteries of their new power forward.

Jordan had spent his time off wisely, all but disappearing from public view while filming the movie *Space Jam*. Pippen and Toni Kukoc competed in the 1996 Summer Olympics, then spent the rest of August recovering from nagging injuries. Ron Harper had surgery, returned to his home in Ohio, and made news only when, upon leaving a gymnasium following some pickup ball with the fellas, he found his car mysteriously riddled with bullet holes. Luc Longley underwent surgery, hung out with the Australian Olympic Team in Atlanta, and finished the offseason with rigorous rehabilitation in Chicago.

Rodman, however, couldn't slow down.

Putting his accelerating career in overdrive, he filmed fifteen episodes for his show on MTV. He filmed *The Colony* with Jean-Claude Van Damme and Mickey Rourke in Nice, France. And just as he had done with Jordan and Pippen, he worked his way onto the marquee. The movie's title was later changed to *Double Team,* better addressing its trio of stars.

He visited Howard Stern and David Letterman, teasing the nation with the promise of an impending marriage. Of course, it was just a publicity stunt, as he showed up the next day at a book signing in New York dressed as a bride.

He opened a nightclub in Dallas with RuPaul, the world's most famous transvestite. He bought an $825,000 oceanfront duplex in Newport, California—plunking down the asking price in cash. He made a cameo appearance on the premiere of the television series "3rd Rock from the Sun." He expanded his endorsement portfolio to ten companies, including a role in Victoria's Secret's "Perfect Silhoutte Bra" campaign. He made a smashing appearance on the MTV Music Awards. He found room on his body for a twelfth tattoo. He had his right nostril pierced during an excursion with musician Tommy Lee, drummer for Motley Crue.

And now, just fourteen weeks after celebrating in the basement of the United Center with the championship trophy, the best basketball team in the world officially reported back to work at their practice facility in suburban Deerfield.

It is the Bulls' policy to invite the media to the affair, which includes access to every player, followed by a team meeting to outline the upcoming campaign. It's done under an implied pecking order, with the reserves lingering on the court and entertaining small audiences, building to the crescendo of grand entrances by Pippen, Jordan, and Bulls coach Phil Jackson.

It is also Rodman's policy to rarely speak when the Bulls are in Chicago. Before a home game, he'll arrive late and find isolation in the secure alcoves of the locker room. After a game, he'll disappear into the weight room, where he works out until most of the media have scurried away under deadline pressure. For the few reporters with time to spare, well, they're left to elicit a few thoughts on Rodman's mad dash to the players' exit.

On the road, where there is no escape, Rodman will sit by his locker, protected by the devices of a loner. He covers his ears with oversized headphones, cranks up a Pearl Jam CD, and stares at the floor.

After a victory on the road, he will speak.

If a camera is available, great. Sound bites are his specialty. They are safe, predictable, and easily manipulated. But he has no use for the print media, where depth is quickly exposed under a string of inquiries.

It is all a calculated approach to protect an image with silence. The less he says, the more mysterious he becomes, the more his rebel persona is fortified. The more he says, the greater the chances of inflicting damage to his own creation.

But on the opening of training camp, he was forced by team mandate to make an appearance.

When Rodman finally emerged from the back curtain of the Berto Center, he was wearing sweatpants, sandals over a pair of white socks, and a neon green blazer. His earrings were big enough to serve as bottle openers. His eyes were hidden beneath a pair of sunglasses, and his newest accessory sparkled from his nose.

This time, however, the gimmick was attached to his left hand. For as he walked to the center of the court to meet a huge gathering of media that had bolted shamelessly from interviews in progress, Rodman was accompanied by a dog. It was a large and loud creature named Aran, a German shepherd equipped with a muzzle.

This, in itself, was a tweak to Bulls management, which had just spent $9 million to re-sign Rodman for the 1996–97 season. For there is a smug sanctity to the Berto Center, ranging from its name (it's dedicated to the late Sheri Berto, a former assistant and confidante to Bulls owner Jerry Reinsdorf) to its emphasis on security (the media never gets to see the Bulls scrimmage, shielded by a mammoth curtain that raises only when practice is over). The walls are a pristine white, the offices and film rooms are upstairs, and under normal circumstances, the basketball court is reserved for employees only. Outsiders are allowed to linger in one area, a narrow hallway connecting the practice court to the locker room.

With the exception of Phil Jackson's dog, a well-behaved creature that occasionally accompanies the coach to practice, the Berto Center was not designed for canines, especially one that had left Rodman's arm and was now barking uncontrollably in one corner of the gym.

Now alone, Rodman stopped at midcourt, and a semicircle immediately formed around him. Microphones and tape recorders were quickly thrust in his face by reporters who jostled for space, and as he witnessed the frenzied ritual unfold at his feet, Rodman offered a knowing smile.

"Welcome back, Dennis," said one television announcer.

No response.

"Whose dog is that, Dennis?" asked another.

"Mine," he replied.

"Boy or a girl?" the television reporter continued.

"It's not my sex partner," Rodman said.

Sadly, this is how most interviews with Rodman begin, even though there were matters of substance to address.

During the offseason, Rodman had expressed a lack of interest in basketball, and said he would probably retire after the upcoming season. He was asked if this was true.

"Yeah," Rodman said. "I think it would be in the best interests not to even bother coming back because all I'm dealing with is the same old bullshit. It's just a different city, a different organization, but the same old bullshit. It's just very difficult. It's just a lot of other things have been bothering me about coming back."

Such as?

"Like the Phil Jackson thing. You have a coach that is making two million dollars, and you have other coaches making four to five million. I think that's really fucked up. I went through that crisis in Detroit with Chuck Daly, and now coming back here to the same shit, it's kind of hard to deal with that.

"I just hate the business aspects of the game. To have a coach that's been here and done what it takes to win—to have four championships in six years—and they treat him like he's nobody. I think that's bullshit. I'm not particularly happy with what's going on here."

For the record, Jackson had just signed a one-year contract for $2.7 million. The negotiations were tough and clearly didn't reward Jackson the way Jordan would be rewarded a few weeks later. But at the time, it made Jackson the highest-paid coach in the league who did not have front-office responsibilities.

Regardless, the antiestablishment rage was Rodman's theme for the evening. Yet following a season in which Rodman was embraced by the city of Chicago, one in which he parlayed his cult-hero status into a rich portfolio of side income, the adversarial tone was strange.

"Don't you want to be here, Dennis?" a reporter asked.

"No, to be honest with you," Rodman said. "I had no time to do anything this summer. It was work, work, work. I'd like to take some time off. Just relax, enjoy myself. I didn't have time to enjoy myself.

"This basketball, dealing with the day-to-day frustrations, is pretty much over for me. It's come and gone. I don't need basketball to make me who I am now. I've got movie deals coming up the next three, four years. That's my next alley. I've got other things going on—movies, sitcoms, my own show—that's going to pretty much keep me occupied. Leaving the game of basketball won't be too hard. This year will be my last year. I want it to be my last year."

As cameras whirred and reporters elbowed for space, Rodman continued to trash Bulls management, driving a wedge into the serenity of a team that had just returned from its honeymoon. The contrast on the court was striking, as was the battle Rodman was purporting to wage within his conscience.

After all, hadn't he finally reached the pinnacle? Hadn't he proved, albeit with a few minor indiscretions, that he could conform within a group once the game started? Hadn't he won his fifth consecutive rebounding title and third championship ring the previous season? Hadn't he finally been rewarded financially, receiving the mother lode from Reinsdorf in negotiations that were suprisingly easy?

"It's not the money," Rodman said. "That's the sick thing. If I didn't come back to Chicago, I probably would've gone somewhere else and played for $250,000 a year."

Yet with Rodman, it's always about the money.

Only this time, it was Jackson's money that mattered.

Or was this just another act in the Rodman circus?

Regardless of content and contradiction, this was just what the media had hoped for—another wave of Rodman antics to fill the great void. The questions continued, mindless inquiries about his experience in filming a major motion picture, his new nose ring, his new tattoo.

As the session ran out of steam, a level-headed female sports broadcaster had one final question for Rodman.

"Dennis, do you think you have us all wrapped around your finger?" she asked.

Rodman didn't look at the reporter, continuing to stare at the floor. But a grin swept across his face.

"Are you?" he said.

"Not in a million years," she answered with a smile.

"Dennis likes sleaze. Dennis likes sex. Dennis likes anything bawdy. It's a good chuckle now and again."

Luc Longley in *Running With the Bulls*

194

"Okay, then," Rodman said flirtatiously, reaching over to touch the reporter. His hand glanced off her elbow, momentarily landing on her breast.

"You just grabbed my elbow," she said. "And the other thing wasn't my elbow."

And he wonders where the mounds of litigation come from?

Fulfilling his commitment, Rodman was escorted to the other side of the gym to have his picture taken for the Bulls' media guide, and then left the court.

Jackson emerged and was told of Rodman's outburst. He was asked if it was a dark omen for the upcoming season.

"No," Jackson said with a devilish grin. "If anything, Dennis is happy to have his life defined for him. We're gonna make it fun for him. He's going to enjoy it."

Would he?

For after bathing in the lights of Hollywood over the summer, it was clear that Rodman wasn't into basketball. He was kicked out of the second exhibition game of the season in Las Vegas. And amidst conflicting explanations, Rodman blew off a home game later in the preseason, raising serious concerns about his focus.

For the game in question, Rodman was nursing a minor injury and wasn't scheduled to play. Yet Jackson learned of his whereabouts only when Rodman had tripped the alarm at the Berto Center, where he had gone to work out by himself while the Bulls were playing thirty miles up the road. It was strange and suspicious, especially since Pippen—also injured and in street clothes—had no problem joining his teammates at the United Center.

Yet the incident was quickly defused by Bulls general manager Jerry Krause, who claimed he had approved of Rodman's absence and blamed the incident on a lack of communication.

Jackson initially said he had excused Rodman from the game, but admitted later that he was simply covering for his power forward.

"I think there are certain standards you have to have as a coach," Jackson said. "You want to treat everyone as fairly as possible because if you start showing favoritism, you destroy the chemistry of the team. There are certain rules, certain fines, and if Dennis crosses the line, he has to know he'll be fined and there will be some action.

"From the standpoint of, 'Dennis has screwed up, let's beat up on Dennis' . . . I don't want to beat up on Dennis. What we're doing right now is important, but in very small letters. All those things start generating as the season goes on. Why should we make a big issue of very small things at this time of the season?"

Clearly, the Bulls organization has succeeded in coddling Rodman. His appetite for self-destruction surfaced the moment he came to camp for his sophomore season with the Bulls, and following three incidents in a seventeen-day span, Rodman had once again tested the managerial waters, probing for breaking points.

The Bulls, particularly Jackson, responded with an olive branch. For just as Rodman was guiding his dog with a leash on Media Night, so too are the Bulls guiding Rodman.

Except there's no muzzle on Rodman, and when he wants to bark in the corner, it is simply treated as background noise. They have tolerated his eccentricities, covered for his transgressions, and for the most part, laughed along with his antics.

You can argue with the methods, but based on Rodman's performance in 1996, you can't deny the results.

Just before the exhibition season ended, the team once again assembled for their annual tip-off luncheon at the Hilton. Rodman's job was to speak briefly and then turn the microphone over to Jackson. But immediately after introducing Jackson to the crowd of 1,500, Rodman bolted from the dais and disappeared into the back room.

He returned moments later, entering the ballroom on a new Harley-Davidson motorcycle. After a short spin around the room, Rodman drove up to the podium. Rodman returned to the microphone and presented Jackson with the motorcycle, which was signed by all of the players.

Jackson was nearly speechless.

Rodman was not.

"I don't want to bust any ass, but the system sucks," Rodman said to his coach. "You didn't get your just due, but fuck 'em."

"He's different. He shows himself totally different than the rest of us. And he does his job. He works hard, and Chicago's that type of town. If you come out and do your job, they respect it. Number ninety-one is not a problem with me, as long as he does his job."

Michael Jordan

And just like that, Rodman had toned down, shedding the rough edges and easing back into the system. The season began with 12 straight victories, ridiculously easy contests in which the Bulls' average margin of victory was 19 points per game. Rodman was a constant force under the basket and a picture of calm outside the arena. There were no more distractions, and a month into the season, the Bulls were 15-1 and on cruise control to another date with destiny.

"You know, the one thing Dennis loves to do is perform," Jackson said. "He loves the competition and the performance it requires. The ninety-four-by-fifty [foot] floor is his stage, and he comes alive at that time.

"Without that, Dennis is . . . I don't know. I could start rattling things off like attention-deficit syndrome. I don't know where Dennis is at [off the court] because he's all over the ballpark. He loves doing things. He loves being here, being there. He's such an active person. I didn't know that such a hyperactive guy could be thirty-five years of age, but he is.

"But I do know what he loves to do. And the way he plays and the way we play collaborate in a good effort. From that standpoint, I think we've gotten the best results out of him."

twenty
MAD SEASON

"I never second-guess what I've done. I never
think, 'Well, maybe I shouldn't have done that.'
Hey, I did it. Accept it."
Dennis Rodman

he fact that Rodman had in-
stantaneously complied was
not lost on his teammates. After an early-season practice, Luc Longley was especially liberal in his praise of Rodman's renewed focus,
noting that he had seemingly shut off all outside distractions.

"He's one hundred percent with us, which is great," Longley said.

Then came a game against the Atlanta Hawks at the United Center in which Rodman displayed a masterful sense of self-control.

After spending much of the night guarding Hawks center Dikembe Mutombo, Rodman began tangling with him in the post. At one point, Rodman pushed the seven-foot-two Mutombo a little too hard, and the emotional center had had enough of Rodman's nagging style of defense.

Just like that, Mutombo was in Rodman's face.

But instead of bumping chests or holding firm in staged bravado, the two began talking. And a minute later, they patted each other on the behind.

"I was talking to him because I really didn't like what he was doing to me," Mutombo said. "Some of it was very stupid. I told him. 'Let's just play basketball. We can't do something silly because both our teams need us.' He agreed, and the game went on.

"Dennis Rodman is a hell of a player."

Yes, Rodman was being good.

Too good, and Jordan sensed as much.

"Leave Dennis alone," Jordan said with a smile. "He's quiet now. Let's keep him that way. He seems to be very focused into doing his job, very respectful. I hope he stays that way."

Before embarking on the first extended road trip of the season, Jackson makes it his annual ritual to hand out books to each of his players. A realist, Jackson knows that maybe a third of the books will actually be opened, and maybe two will actually be read.

Rodman was given a copy of *One Flew over the Cuckoo's Nest,* and the Bulls were on their way.

Yet after three straight victories on the road, the foundation began to crack. On the morning of their first loss of the season, a 105–100 defeat at the hands of the Utah Jazz, Rodman was served with another lawsuit.

This time, Lavon Ankers, a female usher at the Delta Center in Salt Lake City, claimed Rodman touched her in an inappropriate manner after diving into the stands for a loose ball during the 1994 playoffs. Rodman was a member of the San Antonio Spurs at the time.

"This is getting ridiculous," Rodman said. "Everywhere I turn, somebody wants something. It's gone beyond basketball." Indeed, the case was later dismissed.

But later that evening, Rodman played his first poor game of the season. He was ejected for the first time, picking up a pair of technical fouls. He had only 2 points and 10 rebounds and was thrashed by Utah's Karl Malone, who finished with 36 points and 15 rebounds.

"I didn't have my game face on," Rodman said. "It wasn't really exciting to be out there."

It wasn't really *exciting* to be out there? A confrontation against one of the best power forwards in the game and you weren't motivated?

It was a comment that stuck with many of Rodman's teammates.

There was a day off before their next game, a scheduled bout with the lowly Los Angeles Clippers, but even that was trouble for the Bulls. Longley decided to go bodysurfing with teammate Jud Buechler, and despite being a veteran of such activities, Longley ended up on the injured list.

A wave tossed the mammoth Longley into a sandbar, and his left shoulder broke the fall. He limped out of the water in agony, ended up in a hospital, and would miss the next eight weeks with a separated shoulder.

This meant that Rodman had to play center during stretches of the game in addition to his role as power forward, never a climate under which he has flourished.

"Nobody knows what I've been through the last couple of years, and maybe that's the reason I was doing the things I was

doing, to express my feelings, my emotions."

Dennis Rodman

History shows Rodman at his best when he can slip and slide off bigger bodies in the lane, find the cracks and alleys inside where he can dart in, get the rebound, and get out. He has been successful playing center, but only in small doses. And he has never been a force inside when playing with lean centers like Bill Wennington and Robert Parish, which was now the case.

So Rodman began to struggle. Against the Dallas Mavericks, the relatively unknown Chris Gatling scored a career-high 35 points against Rodman. In his first return to San Antonio since being traded by the Spurs, he failed to contain an aging scorer in Dominique Wilkins, who lit up Rodman for 25 points.

In the next two games, a victory over the Milwaukee Bucks to end the road trip and a home win over the Clippers, Rodman was outplayed by the likes of Vin Baker and Loy Vaught.

Couple Rodman's play with his renewed theme of disinterest, and a fracture began to spread in the locker room.

About the same time, there were some unrelated events that helped fuel the fire. In early December, *Forbes* released its list of highest-paid athletes. Jordan was second, having earned $52.6 million in 1996. Rodman ranked ninth, with an income of $12.9 million in 1996.

Pippen was nowhere to be found.

Jordan, in his spare moments, continued to pitch his movie, *Space Jam*, which was dominating the marquee at most theaters. And he had his new line of cologne, which hit the market just in time for Christmas.

Rodman landed on the cover of *Rolling Stone*, and was named one of the ten most "fascinating people" of the year by "20/20," earning a prime-time interview with Barbara Walters. His much-hyped show on MTV was just days away from its season premiere.

Pippen, meanwhile, remains ridiculously underpaid by NBA standards. He was voted one of the fifty best players in NBA history, yet currently ranks as the 131st highest-paid player in the league with a salary of $2.25 million. He is locked into another year with the Bulls, and will become a free agent at the age of thirty-three. He will surely get a nice contract, but a huge windfall may never come.

Pippen surely understands the Jordan phenomenon, and as the years have passed, has grown to appreciate it.

As for Rodman? Well, it's safe to say that Pippen isn't exactly happy with a one-dimensional, self-promoting, cross-dressing player who comes to town and bumps the most versatile small forward in the league down to third billing. There is also a long and dark history between the two players, and all things considered, Pippen's feelings for Rodman were understandable.

Even though Rodman tried to warm the chilly tides between himself and Pippen, it wasn't enough. Rodman was once the enemy, and Pippen still has a scar on his chin to prove it, the result of Rodman's cowardly cheap shot in the 1991 playoffs.

The two existed with mutual, if somewhat uncomfortable, silence in 1996. Rodman tried to make good with Pippen for the 1991 incident, finally apologizing in front of a million people at the Bulls' championship celebration in Grant Park.

Did it have an effect on their current relationship?

"I didn't even hear him," Pippen said.

But was it at least a touching gesture in retrospect?

"Not really," Pippen said.

The situation began to boil over in the next game, a home date with the Miami Heat. The Heat had lost to the Bulls by 32 points earlier in the season, but were maturing quickly under Pat Riley, and entered with 9 wins in the last 10 games.

Just as he did with the Knicks, Riley was steeping the Heat in his own principles, centering on intense, physical defense. And from the start, it was clear that the Bulls weren't ready.

In the first quarter, already struggling on offense, Pippen caught the ball in the post. Two defenders collapsed on Pippen, and Rodman—on the other side of the lane—had an unblocked path to the basket.

Pippen recognized the double-teaming immediately, and fed the ball across his body to Rodman. But Rodman never moved, and couldn't handle the pass. The ball landed in the hands of a photographer.

Following the turnover, an exasperated Pippen clenched his fists and screamed, "Dennis!"

On the bench, Jackson immediately stood up and called for Jason Caffey. The buzzer sounded, Caffey entered the game, and Rodman took a seat on the end of the bench. He untied his shoes and put a towel over his head.

As the game wore on, Rodman hustled, but couldn't catch a break. Trying to control the rebound of a Miami miss, he accidentally tipped the ball into the basket. He did the same thing after halftime, actually scoring four points for the opposition.

He got into a minor altercation with Heat center Alonzo Mourning. He whined to officials. Following a time-out, he punched the ball like you do when serving a volleyball at the company picnic, sending it twenty feet into the air.

Finally, late in the third quarter, a loose-ball foul was called on the Miami Heat. Rodman stood stoically under the basket and began leading the United Center crowd in mock cheers. Referee Bob Delaney ran over to Rodman.

"Stop it," Delaney said.

Rodman began to speak.

"Stop it," Delaney repeated.

Two possessions later, Rodman became entangled with P. J. Brown in the lane, instigating excessive contact. Delaney immediately whistled Rodman for a technical foul, and Rodman landed back on the bench.

The Heat won the game on Dan Majerle's three-pointer with 1.9 seconds left, embarrassing the Bulls, 83–80. It was just their third loss at home in the past two years, and it came at the hands of the hated Pat Riley.

After the game, Jordan lit into Rodman for the first time since they had won a championship.

"Dennis has had a tough week," Jordan said. "He hasn't really been in rhythm. Why? I don't know. Maybe he's lost motivation, from some of the things I've heard.

"Everybody hits a wall during the season. Let's hope this only lasts a week or so and he can get himself focused on some of the basics and positive things this team is trying to accomplish. He hasn't really been playing good, solid defense. The few guys he has faced have played extremely well against him. He hasn't met the challenge emotionally.

"Brown came in and played extremely well and beat Dennis to every loose ball. In the last game, Loy Vaught came in and played extremely well. So he's being challenged, and he's got to elevate his motivation. He certainly shouldn't be bored now because he's certainly getting good tests. He's been outplayed in some respects."

Jordan, in perfect demeanor, was calm as always. But he was issuing a stern warning to Rodman.

"I've been able to find certain challenges every night I step on the court," Jordan continued. "And that's something he's going to have to learn to do. Even at the beginning of the season, when he talked about skipping the whole season and going straight to the playoffs. I used to think that way, but there's a purpose for the regular season, and we have to find it for Dennis. If he hasn't found it over the last couple of nights, he'd certainly better find it in the next couple of weeks."

The Bulls boarded a flight for Toronto, a chance to get well with a victory over the lowly Raptors. But the fog lingered.

This time, Rodman was chewed up by a fourth-year player named Popeye Jones. The Raptors, buoyed by a home crowd of over 33,000 at the enormous SkyDome, hung around all night, and actually led 85–84 with two minutes remaining.

Rodman was whistled by referee Mike Mathis on an obvious charging call, but reacted in disbelief. He waved his arms at Mathis in disgust, but didn't say a word. Referee Bill Spooner, standing at the top of the key, whistled Rodman for a technical foul.

Spooner told Jackson that Rodman had made an obscene gesture. He hadn't, but he was clearly showing up the referee in question. Rodman earned an automatic ejection, having been hit with a technical foul earlier in the game.

As Rodman left the court, he stopped and clapped his hands over his head in unison with the crowd. In the background, Pippen clapped his hands, too.

Following Rodman's exit, the Raptors pulled away, slapping the Bulls with a two-game losing streak. It was Rodman's second ejection of the season, both occurring in Bulls losses.

This time, in front of a horde of reporters and television cameras in the locker room, Rodman snapped.

"You can tell Spooner he can kiss my ass," Rodman ranted. "Did you see me flip him off? I've been trying to be a good boy all year. I don't say shit to the fuckin' referees. I don't know what I should do. I try to stay in this fuckin' league . . . it's ridiculous. It's really ridiculous. I mean, you can't do anything.

"It's sad. It's really sad how this league has turned out to be.

You know, [NBA commissioner] David Stern has got all these fuckin' referees and they got the referees wearing diapers and they can't be fucking men themselves and make a call. I can't believe that.

"I don't know why. Is the league that afraid of Dennis Rodman, that I'm gonna go blow up and kill somebody, break somebody's neck? I don't think so. The league doesn't want to have anything to do with me at all. So basically they can fuck off."

The reporters gathered around Rodman were stunned. And so was the cable television audience in Chicago, which is treated to live coverage of the locker room after every game.

"I don't know what to say about these people, man. They have no heart. They're not men to me. They're pretty much just children to me. These referees, they have nothing.

"Their chains are being pulled by Darell Garretson, the head of the officials, and whatever his fucking name is. That guy who sits up there—Stern, Stern, [Rod] Thorn. David Thorn [sic] is in my ass."

Only then did the cable network pull the plug on Rodman's tirade. But Pippen, in the other corner of the locker room, was just getting started.

"I think Dennis has to conduct himself a little better on the court," Pippen said. "I mean, every time the whistle's blown, he's chasing the ball, doing something with it.

"It builds up frustration within his teammates, so you can imagine how the officials feel. We can't stand there and watch him every play. He has to go out and just play the game and stop doing all those small antics."

Two days later, the Bulls gathered at the Berto Center. The lingering tension made for a riveting practice, though few hung around to talk about it. Jordan and Pippen left without talking to the media, Rodman apologized briefly to the children he offended with his vulgarities, and Jackson pretended to await word from the league office regarding a possible suspension and/or fine.

Yet Jackson had a sermon to deliver, and it centered around a Chicago columnist who reported that Rodman had missed a practice the previous week, "allegedly" without team knowledge. The columnist reported that general manager Jerry Krause would neither confirm nor deny the story, which was indictment enough.

Obviously, there was a leak in the organization, someone who wanted to make Rodman look bad. And in the wake of the incident in Toronto, it did.

"They know that I'm angry at them," Jackson said. "Because something got out to the press yesterday that was nobody's business. We had a guy that missed practice. He had a day off and he was sick and he didn't get up for practice. It's not anybody's business but ours.

"We don't call you guys and ask you if you went to work every single day. I know you guys take a day off every once in a while. So when that kind of stuff gets out and there's a leak in our own family, we are not happy about it."

Jackson was then asked about his reaction to the Rodman explosion.

"I do know it's upsetting. We're not happy that Dennis exacerbated the situation. I think the situation spoke for itself. He was definitely screwed [by the referees]. They were definitely after him. But he didn't have to say what he said."

How about Jordan and Pippen? Did they have to say what they said?

"There are signals that are sent to guys when they're not playing hard," Jackson said. "And usually I send those signals because it's my job as a coach. But our captains . . . they're spokesmen for the team. And if Scottie or Michael make comments about people, even if they're indirect or subtly stated, they carry some weight to them.

That doesn't upset me. That's okay. We're not upset about that, because obviously, guys aren't going to stay motivated for an eighty-two-game season.

"That's what made last year so spectacular. We were capable of doing that, and we were able to win seventy-two of those games. So we're not upset about that. The other things that go on, what happens here on the practice floor, what happens upstairs in our video room or team room, those things are private. That's what we're upset about."

Jackson was circling the wagons. He knew exactly what was going to happen in a matter of hours, and this was his last forum before the organization offered a stunning counterattack. It was his last moment to bond the team back together before the news broke.

He had pacified Jordan and Pippen, confirming their role as troop leaders. He had identified the problem—in-house backstabbing—yet somehow blamed the media for its reaction. This was very similar to the deft touch Jackson used to defuse Pippen's infamous sit-down incident in the 1994 playoffs, when he failed to reenter a game against the Knicks because the last-second shot was asked of—and delivered by—Toni Kukoc.

There was only one thing left, and that was to give Rodman the approbation he needed. It came in gushing, almost laughable torrents.

"I think Dennis is playing hard," Jackson said. "Whether he's attentive all the time or not, I can't tell you that. Like I told Dennis, he is not operating in his high-concentrated level.

"Dennis focuses better than any player I've ever seen. He gets in the locker room, he takes a shower before each game, he puts a towel over his head and he sits there in a meditative fashion which puts him into a ready state in which he plays harder than anyone I've ever seen play this game, including Michael. He plays incredibly hard."

Jackson paused, knowing the risk in such a statement. But Jordan would surely understand, given the situation. He continued.

"He's playing hard, but his focus isn't a full, well-rounded focus, and he's not playing with the offensive aggression he played last year.

"We know he's playing against guys thirty, forty, maybe sixty pounds heavier. It's ridiculous that he has to go up against these guys, but that's the makeup of our team right now. He's our best post-up defender, point blank, and in critical situations, we're asking him to do that. He's still got a big load, but we're not holding him responsible for guys having games. We're not pointing to specific games and saying 'This guy has got twenty points and ten rebounds.' That's not important. What's important is whether we win or lose."

Lecture finished, spin completed, Jackson left the floor.

Four hours later, the Bulls—not the NBA—suspended Rodman. They issued a scathing statement, saying the organization was appalled by Rodman's outburst and would not tolerate such behavior. The suspension was without pay, and the money docked from his check would be donated to charity.

The Bulls had taken the higher ground, preempted the NBA, and lowered the boom on Rodman.

It was a risky maneuver, one Rodman's previous employers in San Antonio had tried, only to get burned by the backfire. They watched Rodman grow even more withdrawn, more surly, more disobedient. They couldn't handle Rodman's indifference, and they grew to despise him so much that losing in harmony was better than winning with such a pain in the ass. And all the while, Rodman could not have cared less.

At that stage in his life, Rodman had refused to give in to authority. It was a battle he would never lose, regardless of personal cost. He was the martyr for personal freedom, the liberated man who needs only inner happiness. It's what made his image what it is today, and don't think he doesn't know it.

So now, after a relatively peaceful honeymoon, the Bulls had also grown tired of Rodman. The coddling was over, the honeymoon a sweet memory.

And just like that, the marriage had gone sour.

#

twenty-one

**"It's not my job to monitor him. That's something
the organization has to do. I feel very reluctant to
step into his world."**

Michael Jordan

Many questions lingered surrounding Rodman's outburst:
Did he know exactly what he was doing? Was he looking for a
break from basketball? Or on the same evening that the "Rodman
World Tour" was unveiled on MTV, did Rodman feel the need to
reinforce his bad-boy image?

The hidden thorn in the situation was the fact that Krause made
a special detour to visit Rodman just before the locker room was
opened, and pleaded with Rodman not to say anything offensive.

"So Dennis knew that his interview was being aired live," Krause said. "That's why I had cautioned him strongly beforehand, 'Now Dennis, don't say anything wrong. I know you're upset. But please be careful about what you say.' "

Jackson met with Rodman immediately after the suspension was handed down, and tried hard to smooth the rough edges. The one thing Jackson didn't want to do was lecture Rodman. He had invested over a year in cultivating his relationship with Rodman, and he could lose the bond in an instant if he began scolding his power forward.

"The reality is, Dennis has been talked to his whole life," Jackson said. "Probably from the time he was a kid he's been talked to by teachers and superintendents and principals and counselors and everything else.

"Dennis knows what he's doing. He's a person that's familiar with his being. What Dennis is working on are some things that will change behavior patterns, and that's what we're trying to deal with right now.

"We've been able to overcome so many controversial issues over the course of the last eight to ten years. I don't think this is anything that will set us back. But we'll see. When he comes back, we'll see what happens."

After the next game, Jordan spoke about Rodman's transgression.

"It's not my responsibility to keep him intact or keep him in line," Jordan said. "He's being paid hefty to go out and do his job, as we all are. We all have to find our motivation in different forms and fashions. In some ways, it's hard, and I can understand some of the things he's going through."

Jordan sensed that Rodman was starstruck, enamored with his growing role as corporate endorser. He noticed that Rodman, who had waited an entire career for such opportunities, was gobbling it all up in monstrous bites.

Rodman had a new business relationship with Kodak, which produced a commercial spoofing his evil image. And he had posed—topless, of course—with a milk mustache for one of those dairy council advertisements.

To Jordan, this was how he lost his focus.

"I've got a lot going on [off the court], more than I've ever had to deal with before," Jordan said. "But I've been able to juggle my way through it. I know what my priorities are: family first, basketball second, and all the other stuff comes third. Nothing interrupts that. That's something I have to stay in tune with and stay conscious of. I advise him to do the same.

"He's taken on a lot. Maybe this is the first time he's ever had to deal with some of these things away from the game of basketball. Maybe it's too much for him, too time-consuming for him."

Then Jordan challenged Rodman's persona rather than his real personality.

"Dennis Rodman has always been the type of guy who says he's in control, and he dictates whatever he wants to do," Jordan said. "He's in control. If that means telling some of these guys or corporations to back off for a while, to let him get his head and his basketball skills back where he wants them, then he should do that. He can't be successful off the court if he's not successful on the court. That's one golden rule of being a spokesperson for a lot of different things."

Clearly, Jordan was saying that Rodman's focus was purely self-centered. And it showed on the court.

"The reason we were a better team last year is rebounding," Jordan said. "It was clearly that, and Dennis was eighty percent of that. The other twenty percent came from the rest of us.

"Now, he's not quite the same. But that's where we have to step in and help him out a little bit. We can't really expect that out of him at his size and weight. He has a big heart, quite naturally, but he's having a tough time trying to put that heart in the right place."

Just like that, Jordan had issued a challenge to Rodman in a very clever manner. He said the Bulls couldn't expect Rodman to excel every night, given his physical limitations, even though he had done so last season. He had questioned Rodman's famous loyalty, and wondered if it had been redirected from the guys in the locker room to his blossoming career in show business.

The words formed a sharp arrow, and were shot to the very center of Rodman's soul:

Hey, we know Dennis was brilliant last season. But we know that he can't exert that kind of energy for another full season. That would be too much to ask of anyone.

They were words that would surely inspire Rodman to once again unleash his maniacal work ethic in order to prove someone wrong.

Jordan had also called upon the bad boy image. Surely such a rebel would never go corporate, right? If he could tell the NBA commissioner to fuck off, surely he could do the same with a few business associates who were sapping his time and energy.

Truth is, no one knew how Rodman would react.

"I don't know what he's going to do," Jordan said. "You just don't know. There are a lot of ifs. Will he come back and act straight and play the game of basketball as we expect him to? We hope so.

"If he doesn't, I'm pretty sure we'll do what we can to maintain our winning tradition here in Chicago. If he's part of that, great. If he's not, I'm sure we're going to have to deal with it when the season is over. We're walking down an alley that not many people walk down."

With the suspension, Rodman extended a streak of mercurial behavior, securing the fifth consecutive year in which he didn't last an entire season.

Silently, his teammates were wondering whether they had been used, whether his incredible, workmanlike effort in 1996 was just part of a game to get Rodman back on his feet financially. And now that he was secure, all they heard was how disinterested he was in basketball, which the statistics proved.

Now he was gone. Would he come back with a new attitude? Had Rodman finally matured, learned from his mistakes, become appreciative of the happiness he had found in Chicago? Or would he continue to drive a wedge through the harmony of the locker room?

As the Bulls boarded their charter for New Jersey, they left with a certain degree of comfort. The morning after the organization disciplined Rodman, he showed up for a brief team meeting and participated in the pregame shoot-around. They told Rodman he was welcome to continue practicing with the team, a move designed to keep him with the program, keep his mind on basketball.

But on the night that the Bulls left town, Rodman was not about to keep a low profile.

The Stone Temple Pilots, a crunching rock band that fits into Rodman's alternative tastes, were making their first appearance in Chicago after a long hiatus, one stemming from the drug problems of lead singer Scott Weiland. As the lights went down in the Rosemont Horizon, Rodman walked onstage carrying an axe, dressed in a grim reaper's costume. He began to shed the outfit, and when the sold-out crowd realized who was introducing the band, there was chaos.

A shirtless Rodman began prancing about the stage, whipping the crowd into a frenzy. And then he took the microphone.

"You know, the NBA is always trying to fuck me," Rodman growled. "But I'm the kind of guy that says, 'Fuck y'all.'

"They're always trying to keep me down, but somehow, I keep rising up."

Just what the Bulls were hoping to hear.

Two hours later, the Pilots were ready for their final encore. Weiland called Rodman back to the stage for a song titled "Sex Type Thing," and Rodman actually sang the second verse.

As the number came to a close, Rodman hoisted Weiland on his shoulders, carrying the singer around the stage. They hugged when the concert ended, hopped into a limousine, and headed to a bar in Chicago.

Later that night, Rodman and the Pilots landed at the Elbo Room, stunning a crowd who had gathered to see a local band. The Pilots got onstage, covering a song from the Sex Pistols. Rodman was next, singing "Wild Thing" while performing a mild striptease. He apologized to the crowd for botching the lyrics, but no one seemed to care.

As the evening ended, Rodman's legend seemed to be hitting new heights in a city already riveted to his every move, but it was presenting the Chicago Bulls and their fans with a strange dilemma:

The crazier he gets the more his teammates become infuriated. Jordan needed eight years to win his first title, and he had strong feelings regarding the class displayed by champions. Rodman was dragging the Bulls into the dirt, prompting Jordan to voice calculated frustration. Krause took the corporate stand, spanking Rodman with a delicate hand. Jackson played good cop, downplaying the crisis and sending verbal roses to Rodman.

But the chasm between Rodman and Pippen continued to grow, and it was clear that Pippen was not going to comply in the coddling.

"I give Michael Jordan the ball so he can lead the league in scoring," Pippen said. "I let Dennis Rodman get his rebounds and get out of his way . . . allow him to pad his rebounding stats. I have to take it upon myself to go after the ball, and not allow Dennis to get a rebound."

Not exactly subtle.

"I don't think I've been harsh on him," Pippen said. "When he comes to work and does his work as well as anybody else on the team, there's nothing to say. But when you don't come to work, then you're letting yourself down.

"We didn't patch the wound up before it got too bad. I think we should have said something to Dennis earlier. We can't look back and say the losses we have should be pointed at Dennis. That is not fair to him. But a big part of those losses, you could say that the guys he was guarding . . . he wasn't giving us the same type of effort that we needed. That's why a lot of this has been building."

And it was far from resolved.

Said Jordan: "He's had a tough time trying to find motivation and challenges at this particular time, which probably led to his outburst. We gave him that inch. Now it's a matter of pulling that inch back into focus a little bit."

But with such heavy stamps of approval from the public, Rodman is further tempted to stretch the boundaries of his persona. What could the grind of regular-season basketball offer Rodman now?

With the suspension, the Bulls were going to get an answer.

"We thought what Dennis did was very inappropriate," Krause said. "It was bad. He caused the organization embarrassment. There are young children that listen to those shows and fans that don't need to hear that language. We felt it had to be stopped, that we had to make a point.

"There's a point where you say, 'Dennis, it can't be done.' It's got to stop. I said that to him last year after he head-butted the official. I said, 'Dennis, it's got to stop,' and he was fine for the rest of the year.

"I respect the hell out of Dennis. But there's a point when an organization has to say, 'That's enough.' "

And start a tiresome cycle all over again.

twenty-two
CAST OFF

"Dennis didn't need Jack Haley."

Michael Jordan

he sparse crowd has filed out of the arena, and Jack Haley sits on the empty bench, watching his children run about the court.

It is two days before Christmas, and Haley's wife and kids have flown in from Los Angeles, joining a man struggling in obscurity, trying to salvage his career in a brewery town buried in the north woods.

But he is once again in demand.

Dennis Rodman had been suspended. The baby-sitter was gone. Who was going to counsel Rodman, and how?

The flowchart led to La Crosse, Wisconsin, where Haley was playing in the shadows, a member of the CBA.

When the news broke, Haley returned to his hotel room to find six messages from writers across the country.

He responded to none of them.

"I'm so sick of this shit," Haley said.

Yes, if there's a casualty of the Dennis Rodman phenomenon, it's Jack Haley.

Haley had been unceremoniously waived by the Chicago Bulls shortly after their victory in the NBA Finals, cast off by an ocean of bad publicity.

He tried to latch on with the Milwaukee Bucks, and almost made the team before getting axed in the final round of roster cuts. But he couldn't retire—not now, not after this—and he ended up with the La Crosse Bobcats, hoping to reclaim both his career and his identity.

It's a steep price to pay for befriending the NBA's unsolved mystery.

"To play nine years, and in one year, have my career and reputation decimated by the media, that all of a sudden I'm no longer an NBA player, that I'm a caddy, that I'm a baby-sitter?" Haley says with disgust. "That gives me a lot of motivation to remind people of who I am."

The public perception of Haley began to change in San Antonio. When Rodman started finding trouble with alarming consistency, Haley would try to defend his friend, the only confidant Rodman had on the team. And as the transgressions continued to get worse, Haley became the media liaison for Rodman, who rarely hung around to give his side of the story.

"I told Jack that he could get away with being Dennis's bo-bo in

San Antonio because nobody cares here," said Bob Hill. "Jack was a big help to me here, and we needed him around.

"But when he went to Chicago, I told him he better break his ties with Rodman the best that he could. Because if he didn't, he was never going to get out of that shadow, and he would never escape that label."

Haley and Rodman were almost simultaneous additions to the Bulls in 1995–96, and while Haley was signed to be part of the team's three-center rotation, the timing spawned many theories.

He knew he was carrying the baggage of Rodman's reputation, but felt secure in returning to Chicago. For he was originally drafted by the Bulls, and in 1988–89, Haley became an instant fan favorite.

It was the first season of real promise in the birth of a dynasty, the first time the Bulls reached the conference finals in the Michael Jordan era. Haley didn't play much, but when he did, it was cause for celebration. He was the poster-boy for blowouts, and whenever a game was securely in the hands of the home team, the Chicago Stadium crowd would begin chanting his name in unison. Inevitably, he would be summoned from the end of the bench, and his mop-up work would be cheered vigorously.

"I was the fan favorite," Haley said. "It was one of the reasons I decided to come back. I had guaranteed offers from Milwaukee for more money, but I wanted to come back to Chicago, to play with Michael Jordan, Dennis Rodman, and Scottie Pippen, to win a championship.

"I sat down with Phil Jackson and Jerry Krause, and they said I would come in as the third-string center, part of the three-headed monster. I was ready to get it on, and I was playing well. And then I got hurt."

Haley suffered an injury during training camp, and it would linger most of the season. And the more he sat on the end of the bench, reduced to cheerleader in a fancy suit, the more his image was tarnished.

Many felt he had been signed just to serve as a sounding board for both Rodman and Jackson, the guy who made sure the Bulls' newest acquisition got up in time for practice.

He would play in only one game during the season, and he was crucified by both fans and the media. He was criticized for not earning his paycheck, and served as a symbol of the implied concerns the Bulls harbored over Rodman.

"And the longer the season progressed, the longer I didn't get a chance to play, the more the players around me started to buy into the media," Haley said. "It was disappointing because they saw how hard I worked in training camp, the enthusiasm I tried to bring to every game. I did everything I could think of to help that team win."

While Haley says he never said a word to Jackson about how to pacify Rodman, the perception snowballed. And to a growing legion of Rodman fanatics, it only furthered the rebellious image. It was cool that this guy was so out of control that he needed a baby-sitter.

Haley endured the ridicule, but his patience finally snapped during the NBA Finals. With Rodman and the SuperSonics' Frank Brickowski engaged in a war of dirty antics that marred the first two games of the series, prominent members of the NBA appealed to Haley, asking that he get his "boy" under control.

"During the NBA Finals, I ran into Del Harris, coach of the [Los Angeles] Lakers," Haley said. "He made a comment to me about the Brickowski thing, about how I better keep an eye on my boy.

"Then [NBA commissioner] David Stern said something to me about it, and that's when it really hit home. Even the NBA was buying into this, and that drove me crazy.

"I was an extremely popular player in Chicago the first time. I loved to go out to the restaurants and bars, to see the people, and they would all say hello. But at the end of that season, it had all changed. It was, 'Look, there goes the baby-sitter.' "

The message, real or not, would continue to be reinforced. After the Bulls returned home, they gathered to distribute their playoff money. Haley was voted only a portion of the winners' share.

He was in the airport, on his way home, when he picked up the newspaper. It said that Haley was snubbed, finally shown how the players really felt about his contributions.

"That was absolutely ridiculous," Haley said. "Did I get a full player's share? No, I did not. Did I get a portion? Yes, I did. Did I get a fair share? Yes, I did. Was I unhappy? No, I was not."

There are also reports that the relationship between Rodman and Haley has changed, that they are no longer close, that Rodman has left his friend to fend for his own.

Clearly, he was no longer needed in Chicago, especially after Jackson developed a wonderful rapport with Rodman. So he left with his championship ring, but it now signifies pain, not achievement.

"Of course, our relationship has changed," Haley said. "Dennis is in Chicago. I'm in La Crosse. Dennis is doing his career, I'm doing mine.

"No one—I mean no one—in this world is happier for Dennis Rodman than I am. He has marketed himself and done a tremendous job. I watch his MTV show and his commercials, and I love it.

"Is our relationship strained? No. Dennis was in L.A. the other day and he called me five times. But do I see him making a trip to La Crosse? No. Do I see myself making a trip to Chicago? No."

Although he claims to have no bitterness toward the Bulls, he is obviously scarred by the ridicule. He didn't show up for the ring ceremony at the start of the 1996–97 season, spurning the invitation. And that's why he's here, playing in a league of outcasts, burning for another chance.

In his first road trip as a member of the Bobcats, he took four flights on twin-propeller planes, including a six-hour layover in which he slept on the floor of Chicago's O'Hare airport.

When they finally landed in South Dakota, the chartered bus broke down. Freezing and full of disgust, the team arrived at a hotel where the marquee advertised rooms for $19.95.

"I've gone from the chartered Bulls airplane, staying at the Ritz Carlton and having police escorts to the arena, to cheap hotels without room service," Haley said. "And the little things, like Gatorade? No. Getting a towel to shower with after the game? That's tough. Now I bring my own bag to the game, which holds all my stuff.

"It's the little things, like a crowd. What did we have tonight, two thousand people? And that was a sparse two thousand."

So how far must a man travel to regain his identity? Haley isn't sure, but he's consumed with thoughts of redemption. Despite his surroundings, he is playing with passion, and after six weeks in the CBA, he was named to the league's All-Star team.

He is waiting for that one phone call, that one last chance to succeed in the NBA . . . on his own terms, without Rodman lurking in the shadows.

"I never thought, after nine years, that I'd have to prove myself again in the CBA. But even if I just remind the people, the general managers and the decision-makers in the NBA, that I can still play this game, it will be well worth it."

A crowning moment?

"If I can sign with the Houston Rockets and go on to beat the Bulls in the Finals," Haley says. "And if I get to play heavy minutes . . . that would be the crowning moment."

Haley is done talking, and although he carries a brain full of memories and secrets of a friendship that burned him in the long run, he will not discuss Dennis Rodman.

"You have to understand," Haley says. "I've had it up to here with that baby-sitter stuff."

In the stands, one of the Bobcats' assistant coaches is talking to a man and his young daughter. The conversations turns to Jack Haley, and the assistant coach relays some information.

"You know, he and Dennis Rodman are like this," the coach says, crossing two of his fingers. "They're best friends."

The little girl suddenly perks up.

"Really?" she says in awe. "Dennis Rodman is *sooo* cool."

Yes, Jack Haley is in for the fight of his life.

"That's why I'm here," he says. "I would really like to retire and not have that be my legacy. It's going to be extremely hard to erase all of that."

Three weeks later, Haley would be named a CBA All-Star.

A week after that, he was signed by the New Jersey Nets.

He was back in the NBA.

twenty-three

NEW BEGINNING

"I'm a grown man. I know exactly what I'm doing."

Dennis Rodman

The crowd at the United Center had filtered in earlier than usual, all awaiting the return of Dennis Rodman, and a heavy buzz hung over the court. Rodman had served his two-game suspension for cussing out the commissioner and referees, and the penalty had become an event, a milepost in a long season. The curiosity and concern centered on how he'd react in his return against the Charlotte Hornets, if he had reformed or if his unruly behavior was just an omen of things to come.

He was the last player to arrive at the United Center, and surely, such timing was not a coincidence. Wearing a floppy fur hat and sunglasses, Rodman stared at the floor as he walked down the hallway, oblivious to the bodyguard at his side. And in an awkward moment, Rodman made it to the locker room at the same time as Jerry Krause, who was approaching from the opposite direction.

Their eyes never met, and Krause slowed up at the door, deferring to Rodman.

While his statistical line would be celebrated—a 25-rebound performance in an 87–82 victory—it was a surly display, and his trademark enthusiasm was missing. He was clearly agitated with the referees, and after one call, he waved off an official four times in succession—the kind of gesture that had led to his ejection, and ultimately, the suspension.

But on this evening, the officials were obviously cutting Rodman some slack, sort of a makeup call for the furor that arose out of the fiasco in Toronto. After the game, Jackson was asked why Rodman, in the wake of a two-game suspension, would immediately revert to his combustible demeanor.

"Addictive behavior," Jackson said. "As we go through the season, I think we're just going to have to continually ask for more behavioral control on his part."

Two days later, the Bulls gathered at the Berto Center to prepare for a game against Shaquille O'Neal and the Los Angeles Lakers. It was O'Neal's first game against the Bulls since he left the Orlando Magic, and the first since the Bulls' four-game sweep in last year's playoffs. O'Neal had been rendered useless then by Rodman's athleticism and agitation, and now he was in the mood for revenge.

It was bad enough that Rodman had outplayed and criticized O'Neal during the playoffs. But over the summer, on a night when O'Neal hosted a party celebrating his new record label, Rodman was debuting his new club in Dallas. And he furthered the feud with another pointed barb.

"I'm one of the most intimidating players out there, a person a lot of players do not want to see."

Dennis Rodman

"Well, he's twenty-five years old, young, full of it, and good luck," Rodman said. "Good luck in all your success. But before you step into the ring with the big boys, you've got to understand the game. Understand the game, how to play the game and deal with the fact that, hey, no matter how big you are, your ass is going to fall."

Jackson was leery of Rodman's mind-set, not to mention O'Neal's. The Lakers center had promised to get "mean" during the confrontation, and with Luc Longley still out of the lineup, things could get ugly.

Rodman had to get through this game unscathed, so Jackson made a decision: He would defend O'Neal with the combination of Bill Wennington, Robert Parish, and Dickey Simpkins. Rodman would concentrate on the Lakers' Elden Campbell and stay away from O'Neal.

But a funny thing had happened on the way to the Berto Center. Rodman claimed to have been struck by inspiration, filled with a newfound motivation.

He was a changed man.

"Coming to practice today, I started thinking," Rodman said. "And you know, I think I'm really getting back into the swing of the game, so I hope it's just the start. I hope people haven't gotten down on me and turned their backs on me. Like I say, 'I'm not going to let you down, so don't let me down.'

"I have to have something that's going to be very challenging. I can't kid myself and say I'm having a great time if I'm not. A lot of people kid themselves in this league, saying they're playing for the fun when they're just playing for the money. I'm not playing for the money. I'd rather sit out and try to get my head together, and I think this past week has been pretty good for me."

Just like that, Rodman had laid down a heavy commitment to the Bulls, almost a promise to stay focused for the rest of the regular season. This type of conformity seemed unprecedented, especially this early in the season.

He wouldn't reveal his new source of motivation, but admitted that the public reprimands from Jordan and Pippen had played a part.

"It was the truth," Rodman said. "I haven't been playing hard. I haven't been doing the things necessary for the team, and I think they knew that. So they spoke out.

"I won't get mad at them for that because they know what's going on. Those guys are too smart, too educated. I don't blame them at all. I put all the blame on myself."

Rodman was now complying with all of the Bulls' wishes. He wasn't going to file a grievance over a two-game suspension without pay, and he was shouldering a significant amount of responsibility—as much as he could without losing his rebellious image.

"The money has been given to charity, and I think that's great," Rodman said. "I won't take that back. It's better than giving it to the fucking NBA. But I'm going to fight for the fact that they've been messing with me.

"I'm just going to file a grievance saying there's a conspiracy out there toward Dennis Rodman this year. They are anticipating any little thing I do, and they just watch me.

"But the money? That's going to help some people who need some things. Me, I don't need anything. I can go out and buy anything I want. But I know what it's like, being a kid and not having anything for Christmas. Besides, I owe the people something for what happened. I'm just hoping that they'll stick behind me."

Maybe for the first time since he roared into town, he felt the unconditional support slipping away. Maybe he had listened to Jordan, who suggested that his bridge to Hollywood had to be anchored to his athletic career. Maybe he sensed that he had finally pushed the public too far. And maybe he conceded to the most repulsive notion of all—that despite all the obscene bluster, Dennis Rodman really needed the NBA.

Either way, the Lakers came to town the following day and did the unthinkable. They began hammering the Bulls from the opening tip-off, and O'Neal was unstoppable, scoring at will over Wennington, Parish, and Simpkins.

The Lakers were en route to a telling blowout, but during a time-out midway through the third quarter, Rodman did something strange.

He spoke.

He asked Jackson to let him guard O'Neal straight up, and without any other options, Jackson relented.

In the final 23 minutes, Rodman held O'Neal scoreless. The Lakers' monstrous center simply disappeared in the offense, attempting only three shots during that time span. And the Bulls overcame an 18-point deficit in the fourth quarter to prevail in overtime.

Once again, he had bested O'Neal, who couldn't contain his frustration.

Near the end of the game, Rodman had tracked down a loose ball, colliding with the Lakers' Jerome Kersey. Rodman began to signal for a time-out, but was bumped by Kersey. After regaining his balance, Rodman took a menacing step toward Kersey. O'Neal quickly jumped into the fray, and pushed Rodman in the chest.

Rodman again regained his balance, and charged at O'Neal. But he was intercepted by both Jordan and Pippen, and the scene was fascinating.

Jordan grabbed Rodman by the throat with both hands, while Pippen grabbed him around the chest and tackled him to the floor. When they arose from the court, both Pippen and Rodman were smiling in unison.

Doc Rivers, who was broadcasting the game for the TNT network, began lauding Jordan and Pippen for their actions. And he praised Rodman for calling a time-out, avoiding being fouled and sent to the free-throw line where he could hurt the Bulls.

At the same time, veteran Lakers announcer Chick Hearn offered a different analysis:

"Stupid Rodman!" he barked.

When the game was over, Rodman was ecstatic. It was just like the playoffs, and just what he needed. It was a game that displayed his courage and worth, a chance to get down and dirty for both his team and his city. It was also carried to a nationwide audience of three million homes, the fourth-highest-rated regular-season game broadcast on cable in history.

Rodman knew he was playing on a big stage, and knew he had just recaptured much of his fan base. He was corralled by a TNT reporter as he bounced off the court and asked about his stifling defense.

"People may say Dennis Rodman is this or that," he said. "But they can't deny he's a hell of a basketball player."

twenty-four

ALL EYES ON ME

"Dennis is *Heyoka* . . . a backwards-walking

person in society."

Phil Jackson

As Rodman raced off the court, there was an intriguing possible reason for the sudden change in his demeanor.

With his suspension, he was once again on a short leash, just like the noose that had tightened around his neck following the head-butting incident last season. And with his strange behavior in his first game back against the Charlotte Hornets, he prompted critics to shake their heads in disbelief, wondering if Rodman would ever learn.

> ## "Some people see me on the streets and really appreciate what I do. I hear a lot of people say, 'You're one of us.'"
>
> ### Dennis Rodman

But what he had done could be construed as pure genius from a marketing standpoint. Once again, he had drawn the focus of an entire season squarely on his shoulders, and was once again the center of attention. He was the guy who could blow up at any moment, and if that happened, Rodman's days in Chicago could be over. Would the Bulls tolerate another fiasco, or like the Spurs, would they decide to cut their losses?

He had pushed the boundaries of acceptance to the limit, only to pull up on the reins at the last minute.

And now, all eyes were fixed on Dennis Rodman.

Just the way he likes it.

Rodman was also playing another role to the hilt. He was allying himself with the elder generation of superstars who were becoming more and more disenchanted with the younger breed of players. Like Jordan, Charles Barkley, and Karl Malone, Rodman began taking the state of the game to task, blaming attendance ills and attitude problems on a lack of respect shown by a majority of the NBA's future stars.

Just days after proving his point about O'Neal, the Bulls arrived in Philadelphia for a game against the Philadelphia 76ers and rookie sensation Allen Iverson.

Iverson's phenomenal talent was matched with extreme cockiness, and before tip-off, he was yapping at Jordan, telling the icon that he didn't have to respect anyone.

Later in the game, Iverson and Rodman would get acquainted. After a foul was whistled on Iverson in the third quarter,

Rodman came up to the rookie and playfully tapped him on the behind.

"Don't touch my butt," Iverson snapped.

Rodman nodded in mock understanding, but as the two ran upcourt, he again patted Iverson on his behind. Iverson immediately began pointing at Rodman, and had to be restrained by his teammates.

In the final minute of the game. Rodman gave Iverson a forearm push as the two were battling for a loose ball, and Iverson was sent sprawling to the floor. Rodman was nailed with a technical foul, and again, the two had to be separated.

"I just wanted him to come in the lane so I could hit him," Rodman said. "I didn't want to hurt him, but I wanted him to make sure that he knew you can't come in here, talk all that stuff and not expect to get hit.

"You've got to respect the game and respect the players you're playing against. He thinks he's God. G-O-D. He thinks the court is his street, his playground, and he can do anything he wants and say anything he wants. It's sad. It's very sad.

"He's very talented, but he has to understand, it's not all about individual talent. He thinks it's street ball out there. He had thirty-two points, but he's out there shooting, how many times, forty?

"One of us will have to flatten him on his butt. I think that's what most young players coming into the league need, someone to straighten their butts out. But they don't know anything about the game."

In his own way, Rodman was also trying to reestablish an unspoken bond with Jordan and Pippen. In the first meeting between the two teams in November, it was Iverson and Pippen who had gotten into a heated exchange.

Pippen had tired of the rookie's chatter, and began baiting him, telling Iverson that he wasn't a true point guard, that he shot the ball too much, etc. Eventually, Iverson had worn thin, and he confronted Pippen. And when Jordan stepped in to separate the players, Iverson shot back at Jordan.

"Get the fuck out of here," Iverson said.

So now Rodman was stepping in for his teammates, and providing the kind of retribution that the classy Jordan would eschew. For Rodman, it was the kind of role he had grown to love in Detroit, the voice and muscle of team protector.

While Jordan refused to blast Iverson for his lack of respect, Rodman did the dirty work, providing the scathing commentary. Certainly, the words would get back to Pippen and Jordan, words that would help dissolve the distance between Rodman and the Bulls' dynamic duo.

"These young kids have these big contracts and they have this avenue where they can do pretty much what they want to do, and the league is letting them," Rodman continued. "The young players that come out of college today, most of the guys can't even spell their own names.

"You hear guys like, 'C'mon, c'mon, c'mon.' Excuse me, hello, we have a vocabulary here. They need to stay in school and understand the game of basketball. I see some of these rookies and they can't even talk. They think their money does the talking. It's more than that.

"This game is totally different than it was ten years ago. Guys used to come in ten years ago and not get the big contracts. They used to play hard to be respected. Now, it's like the guys don't give a damn.

"It's hurting the game right now. I mean, you have individual instead of team play right now. It's more individuals, more stats, it's more who can do what against who instead of team by team.

"You know, David Stern is doing a great job."

Iverson also symbolized another challenge for Rodman. If this was indeed his final year in the league, a season in which pretentious youth littered the NBA landscape, he must again prove that his savvy and experience were far more valuable than unhoned skill. He must show that his championship pedigree would always prevail, and to do that, he must embark on the kind of ruthless strategy that only Rodman can implement: a war of attrition, to bust ass for the rest of the season and end his career with an exclamation point.

In the three games since Rodman had returned from his suspension, the Bulls outrebounded their opponents 156–131. Rodman had played 47 minutes against the 76ers, hauling down 18 rebounds and scoring 12 points. After the game, Jackson extended another heaping plate of praise to Rodman, again placing him in historical perspective.

"He can play harder for longer minutes than anyone I've ever seen," Jackson said. "He loves the long minutes, he actually gets better as the game goes on."

But Rodman was just getting started. On Christmas night, the Bulls throttled the rapidly maturing Pistons, 95–83. Rodman again dominated, finishing with 22 rebounds, 11 points, and 7 assists while playing 46 minutes.

For both Jordan and Pippen, it was time to open their arms and let Rodman back into the family.

"He seems to be focused," Jordan said. "I think he respects us to the point where he comes out each and every day to do his job. He had a tough time trying to find a sense of motivation, and it's understandable. When you get to a point where you're one of the great players, great rebounders, it's tough to try to find a sense of motivation. You have to dig deep within yourself to try and find that.

"I've done it, Scottie has done it, other players have done it. I think that's something that even he has learned to improve on."

One locker away, Pippen was also in a forgiving mood.

"I think he realized that we didn't want to put up with [the antics] that early," Pippen said. "It's tough enough that we were starting to struggle as a team. With Luc out of the lineup, it finally caught up with us. And then to have one of the best players on the team start to go AWOL . . . I mean, it makes it very difficult, especially when you're trying to lead a team to be a great team like we were last season. You can't put up with that this early in the season."

twenty-five
CRUISE CONTROL

"In reality, he does nothing for anybody but Dennis Rodman."

an NBA general manager

lexis Rodman is fidgeting in the basement of the United Center, fighting back a case of the yawns.

She is now eight years old, and it's easy to see why the thought of her can make her daddy cry. With light brown skin and a head full of bushy brown curls, she is the picture of innocence and beauty.

She is holding a Dennis Rodman jersey tucked neatly over her arms, and just waiting. And waiting. And waiting.

"Why is he always the last one out?" she says to no one in particular.

Her mother, Annie Bakes Rodman, is standing against the facing wall, and she offers a smile of understanding to the child.

His teammates have all left the building, but Rodman is still in the back of the Bulls' locker room, completing his postgame weight-lifting regimen. And things are going too well to mess with the ritual.

Rodman had just hosted a New Year's Eve party for the city of Chicago, an affair that attracted three thousand people to a ballroom overlooking Lake Michigan. And while the host showed up late and left shortly after delivering the traditional countdown to midnight, the party served its purpose.

Over three thousand people paid admission to attend the bash, got a glimpse of Rodman and a story to tell their friends. Rodman showed off his newest costume—an elaborate cross of King Tut and Cleopatra, complete with a fully sequined gold-and-purple cape and a price tag of $10,000. And a lineup of Filter, a Chicago-based in-dustrial music group, and Candlebox, a headliner from Seattle's sec-ond wave of grunge, gave the affair a big-time feel.

While Rodman desired to hang out with his small group sectioned off in a narrow corner of the balcony overlooking the side of the stage, he mingled a bit, and was the subject of countless photographs as he posed in front of two enormous gold and red velvet thrones.

"Dennis just likes to have fun. He's high energy and he doesn't sleep much. He had a bad marriage and puts no stock what-soever in relationships or marriage. His whole world is rapid turnover without re-sponsibility."

Luc Longley in *Running With the Bulls*

The most revealing part of the evening was the fact that three of his teammates—Luc Longley, Steve Kerr, and Jud Buechler—also showed up to rage with Rodman. Although Longley had since become tight with Rodman, the presence of Kerr and Buechler was a further testament to Rodman's current standing.

And just two nights later, with Alexis in attendance, Rodman had returned to his own personal throne.

He had 22 rebounds and 10 points in a win over the Orlando Magic, overtaking the league rebounding lead for the first time in the season. He had already caught and passed Charles Barkley, ending a silly war of words.

After snaring 33 rebounds in the opening game of the season, Barkley would lead the league for the first three weeks. And he scoffed at the title, his way of discounting Rodman's accomplishments.

"If all I had to do was concentrate on rebounding, I'd lead the league in rebounding, too," Barkley said.

Rodman heard of Barkley's comments and issued a dare. If Rodman overtook Barkley and won his fifth rebounding title, Barkley would have to wear a dress. Rodman waited for Barkley's response, but it never came.

He overtook Barkley two weeks before Christmas. And now, after another dominating performance against the Magic, he had surpassed the Nets' Jayson Williams as well.

In the first quarter of the game, he grabbed 14 rebounds, tying the Bulls team record set by Clifford Ray in 1972. Nine of his rebounds were on the offensive end.

"They work so hard to contain Scottie and Michael," Kerr said. "They miss a shot, and you can almost see them say, 'Yes,' Then Dennis comes away with the ball, and they have to start all over again. That's one of Dennis's great qualities—he demoralizes an opponent."

Rodman also scored nine points in the third quarter, displaying a burst of offensive moves, left-handed layups, and turnaround jump shots.

He couldn't have scripted the night any better, and when Rodman finally emerged from the locker room, Alexis started to bounce with excitement.

"There he is," she said.

"Oh," said her mother. "I didn't even recognize him."

Rodman sauntered down the hallway, wearing his baseball hat and sunglasses, stopping for a brief interview. Then he grabbed his little girl by the hand and began to walk.

Annie Bakes Rodman had moved to the periphery of his entourage, and stood against the wall.

"Good game, Dennis," she said.

Rodman ignored her, and continued to walk slowly, hand in hand with his daughter, out into the evening.

"When I see her, you realize basketball isn't important," Rodman said.

The next afternoon, a reporter is waiting in the lobby of the Omni Hotel in Chicago. He had spoken to Annie two hours earlier, and she sounded eager to talk, eager to dissolve a few myths surrounding her famous ex-husband.

But now she is stuck in the hotel room waiting for Dennis to pick up Alexis. He is two hours late, she says, and her little girl is beginning to pace the room.

"She doesn't think he's coming," she said. "Now you see what I have to put up with all the time."

On the phone, she pauses briefly.

"Did you see the thing last night?"

Sure. He walked out of the arena holding hands with his daughter.

"It was all an act," she says. "All for show."

Another hour later, Rodman's unmistakable truck pulls up outside the hotel. Except Dennis isn't in the truck. One of his friends has come to pick up Alexis and take her to Gold's Gym, where Dennis is working out.

Except Alexis won't get in the truck with a stranger.

Finally, Rodman calls Annie, and she takes Alexis to the gym herself. When she talks to the reporter on the phone four hours later, she apologizes profusely.

"It's ridiculous," she claims. "I wouldn't even have come out here this weekend except that Dennis has promised to help me out financially."

They plan to meet the following day, but Annie Bakes Rodman simply disappears.

She would sell her side of the story for $150,000, signing a deal to write a tell-all book titled *Worse Than He Says He Is: Off the Court with Dennis Rodman.* She would detail the violent nature of their seven-year relationship and the sexually transmitted diseases she allegedly acquired from Rodman.

Whether Rodman was physically abusive to his former wife is unknown. But she isn't the first to charge him with passing along a sexual disease.

In 1995, an Atlanta Hawks dancer named Lisa Beth Judd claimed she had met Rodman in December 1993. She accused Rodman of infecting her with herpes, saying he knew he had the virus before the two engaged in unprotected sex.

While a jury deliberated less than four hours before clearing Rodman of any wrongdoing, Rodman admitted in a videotaped deposition that while he had tested negative for herpes in 1988, he was diagnosed with the virus in March 1993.

Regardless, the book is her revenge, her chance to catch the wave of Rodman controversy and ride it in. But for all the bluster, the anger inside Annie Bakes Rodman doesn't gibe with her actions.

When she had shown up at the United Center, she was dressed for the occasion, filling a pair of black leather pants that provided a stark contrast to her blond spiked hair. She seemed once again entranced with her husband's notoriety. She was escorted into the building with her daughter, and led to the room designated for players' families. And she had registered at the hotel as Anicka Rodman, a name that was once reality for eighty-two days, but no longer.

At least to Dennis Rodman.

"She wants me back, but I don't want her back," Rodman said during the 1996 playoffs. "I could sue her for making a lot of false charges against me, saying I beat her and other stuff. But this would just give her more publicity."

Now her weekend in Chicago was over, and Annie Bakes went home with her daughter in tow and her story intact, waiting for the next time she must give custody to her ex-husband.

Was she running to protect a man whom, after all the screaming and acrimony, she still loved?

Or was she running from her own history?

It is, indeed, a damaged relationship forged by two misfits, an accident waiting to happen.

And less than a month later, Annie Bakes Rodman would tell a newspaper of a stunning yet predictable twist in their fractured marriage: Alexis Rodman had recently become angry on the playground at school, and reacted by striking a classmate. When questioned why she did it, her answer was terrifying:

"Well, that's what my daddy does," she said.

Alexis Rodman is now undergoing anger-management counseling.

Although his daughter was gone, Dennis Rodman remained on a major roll. The Utah Jazz came to town, and it would be the complete opposite of their first meeting earlier in the season, when Karl

Malone thrashed Rodman, sending the Bulls' forward spiraling down a path of disinterest.

Rodman finished with 16 rebounds and 6 points. While fleshing out his statistics in the second half, Malone made only one of eight shots in the decisive first half.

"Like I said, I'm back in the groove, back in the flow of things, and the vibe is there," Rodman said. "It just naturally came back to me. Everything is where I want it to be. I have to get the respect back from the people of Chicago, and once I get that, everything will be running smoothly."

In the next four days, Rodman divorced Nike as his shoe manufacturer, and signed a $2.5 million deal to be the marquee endorser for Converse.

And he turned in season-bests for points (16) and rebounds (26) in a victory over the Milwaukee Bucks, one made even more memorable when Rodman traded in his role of agitator for peacemaker.

Late in the game, Michael Jordan was driving for a layup when he was elbowed in the head by the Bucks' Armon Gilliam. Jordan took exception to the contact, and began to walk toward Gilliam when Rodman intercepted him. He wrapped his arms around Jordan, defusing a volatile situation.

Things were getting very strange, and Rodman was only warming up.

Next up were the Houston Rockets, who came to Chicago in a game hyped as a possible preview of the NBA Finals. For Rodman, it was a chance to go head-to-head with Barkley, and these kinds of challenges don't come around very often.

Early in the first quarter, Rodman was slapped with a technical foul, and Barkley clapped his hands in approval. When the period ended, Barkley again started clapping his hands, laughing and pointing a finger at Rodman.

"You're in for a long night," Barkley said.

"A long night, huh?" Rodman replied.

The Bulls would go on to a 110–86 romp over the Rockets, and Barkley had never been so wrong in his life. Rodman finished with 18 rebounds and scored 8 points, while his defense rendered Barkley useless.

Barkley barely matched Rodman's scoring total of 8 points, and he made just 2 of 11 shots.

"Dennis just kicked our butts," Barkley said. "He outplayed me. It's as simple as that."

And then came the crowning moment. In the next game against the Washington Bullets, Rodman recorded the 10,000th rebound of his career, becoming only one of twenty-four players ever to reach the barrier.

The game was stopped after Rodman reached the milestone, the public address announcer rattled off his list of accomplishments, and the United Center crowd responded with a standing ovation.

Rodman buckled. So touched by the gesture, Rodman put his hands on his knees, hung his head down and began to cry. But he quickly composed himself, waved to the crowd, and the game resumed.

"It's something you work so hard to get, you finally get it, and you have to appreciate it," Rodman said. "You know, people go to work nine to five, and when something good comes to them, they show it. I've done the dirty work for many years, and something good came out of it.

"A lot of places, I wouldn't have gotten [an ovation] like that, but Chicago realizes what I do and what I've done. And it feels good that I can give back to the people.

"I get paid to do a job, I get paid to entertain people. And hopefully, every time I take the floor, I can provide more and more excitement for the people. I've got to earn my money somehow."

Rodman was doing more than just earning his money. He was

in the midst of a sensational roll, stacking consistently brilliant performances on top of each other with marked intensity. He was doing what he had promised his city and his teammates, and the Bulls were unstoppable. He was going to make it very difficult to again be overlooked for the All-Star Game, whoever had to make the decisions. Because he deserved it, and that opinion was strongly endorsed by both Jordan and Pippen.

On his way out of the stadium after making NBA history, Rodman found a massive wave of cameras and reporters waiting in the hallway. They moved along with him, bumping into walls, walking backwards, doing what they had to in order to get Rodman on tape. He stopped at the area where media was no longer allowed, and began to reflect on his career.

"I've told myself over the years that I'm surprised I'm still here," Rodman said. "But the hard work paid off. You have to look at me. I'm a late bloomer. The first three or four years in the league, I wasn't averaging anything. The last six or seven years is where I really paid the price. I'm the perfect example that you don't have to be number one, the chief honcho, to make it big.

"It's just a matter of desire, the will to do it, to get in there and bust heads with all the big guys. I'm not afraid of anything."

Finally, Rodman was asked about the next game:

"The Timberwolves are the Timberwolves," Rodman said. "We have to go to cold-ass Minnesota and go play."

Rodman disappeared, the cameras were turned off, and the media headed back down the hallway, trying to restore their dignity. The Bullets' Tim Legler was walking the same hallway when he noticed the mad rush that accompanies Rodman out of the building, and he smiled.

"I thought they were moving Hannibal Lecter," he said.

Yep, and he was on his way to Minnesota.

twenty-six

LAND MINE

"He's a life wasted."

Utah Jazz president Frank Layden

erry Krause was sitting in his living room, enjoying the blowout on television, when the entire season flashed before his eyes.

"Oh my God," Krause exclaimed.

In one moment of impulsive rage, Dennis Rodman had once again snapped, exploding in the face of harmony and placing an entire mission in jeopardy.

Late in the third quarter in a meaningless game against the Minnesota Timberwolves, Rodman was fighting for a loose ball when his momentum carried him out of bounds. He tripped on the leg of a photographer, nearly spraining his ankle before tumbling to the floor.

Rodman paused for a moment, spotted a cameraman in front of him, and unloaded.

He delivered a fierce kick that appeared to land on the inner thigh of Eugene Amos, a forty-eight-year-old cameraman who wasn't even the cause of Rodman's tumble. Amos reacted in shock, shouting at Rodman. And after a delayed reaction, he doubled over in pain and had to be removed from the arena on a stretcher.

"He had a camera on the court where it shouldn't have been, and any athlete will tell you that's their career," Rodman complained. "I was aiming at his camera. I wasn't trying to kick him."

The game resumed, but the implications were obvious and severe. After the game ended, Rodman delivered another postgame tirade, this time attacking the Timberwolves' Stephon Marbury as another young player without a clue, but his anger was clearly misdirected. He tried to downplay his assault on Amos, laughing about the incident while standing at his locker.

"It's one thing to be hurt," Rodman said. "But don't pretend you're hurt more seriously than you are. It was a little bit dramatic to me. Maybe I'll send him roses on the floor—'Love, Dennis.' "

The next day, Amos surfaced on the streets of Minneapolis, and a few television stations were waiting for his side of the story.

"I grew up with that team," Amos said. "This is the greatest franchise in history, as far as I know. They're the greatest, the whole team, and I love them all—except one.

"He kicked me in the groin, and I went into, like I don't know— some kind of shock. But it was a very painful situation. I've been to two doctors so far. I've had two X rays. I've been examined. I have problems."

So did Rodman.

Whether Amos was seizing an opportunity or dealing with a substantial injury was not relevant. And while the abundance of courtside photographers poses a nightly nuisance to NBA players, especially when the Bulls come to town, Rodman's behavior was the real issue.

For no one else in the league had reacted toward a courtside reporter with such venom, and players were stumbling over cameramen on a regular basis. And like it or not, those photographers served a purpose in the NBA's grand marketing scheme.

Once again, the NBA had to take a stand, and the Bulls braced for the worst. Stern and Thorn convened to discuss the matter. They had given the Bulls a free pass following Rodman's expletive-laced tirade toward Stern and league officials earlier in the season, allowing the team to set their own discipline. Now it was hammer time, and two days later, they relayed their decision.

"I think the NBA is going to ruin itself in the next three, four, five years."

Dennis Rodman

Rodman would be banned indefinitely, with a minimum suspension of eleven games. Over the All-Star break, he was to meet with Stern, and would have to tell the commissioner in his own words why he was no longer a menace to the game of basketball.

And here was the kicker, if you pardon the expression: Rodman would be required to attend league-mandated counseling, which was the ultimate slap in the face. Rodman had been suspended under similar conditions in the past while in Detroit and San Antonio, but was always allowed to visit his personal psychiatrist.

It would also cost Rodman a fortune. He would lose over $1.2 million in salary during the suspension, and was docked an additional $25,000 by the league. And with the lengthy suspension, he lost all of his incentive clauses with the Bulls, all bonuses based on games played.

It was time for Stern to put his foot down, and when he did, it landed right on Rodman's throat.

It was the second-longest suspension in NBA history, second only to the sixty-day ban issued to Kermit Washington for his infamous sucker punch that shattered Rudy Tomjanovich's face.

It was also a heavy statement, an ominous warning from the league offices that no one is bigger than the game, particularly Rodman. And it was the strongest challenge Stern ever issued in his long-running battle with Rodman, almost a dare to walk away from the game.

"We can't control him," Michael Jordan said. "We all know that. The system is trying to control Dennis, and if Dennis wants to change, then Dennis will change."

Although the Bulls pushed forward, it was clear that the situation had begun to grate on his teammates. They were supremely disgusted with the never-ending distractions, and just as had happened with Rodman's former teammates in San Antonio, their patience was at an end.

Now they wanted to win in spite of Rodman, to make their own statement. Jordan, in particular, saw a challenge to restore some dignity to the organization, one that had once prided itself on character and grace.

"Life goes on," Jordan said. "We're sad he's not part of the team, but we have to survive until he possibly comes back, and that's it. We can't change what the league has done now.

"If he pays his dues, we take him back, and we move on. But we can't sit back until All-Star break and see what happens. We have to move forward."

Four days after the suspension, Rodman left the Bulls, returning to California. Although he was eligible to practice with his team, the Bulls didn't want the accompanying distractions, and let him go with their blessings.

Back at home in Newport Beach, Rodman moved quickly to clean up the shrapnel left in his wake. He paid Amos $200,000 to drop all legal charges, and assured Bulls fans that he would be back.

But was the damage permanent? Had Rodman finally worn out his welcome with his cultlike following? Even in Chicago, there were signs that the fans had had enough of Rodman—enough of his act, his boorish behavior, his clamoring for attention.

Had the antihero phenomenon run its course?

"He remains what he long has been," said NBC's Bob Costas on national television. "Someone who'd have to move up several notches to qualify as a fool. If he stands for anything at all, it's an unwitting symbol of how crass and empty the whole concept of who's worthy of our attention, and in some cases our adulation, has become.

"His act is so predictable and uninspired that the only thing that remains truly annoying about the Rodman situation is the number of people who persist in the belief that Dennis Rodman somehow stands for something."

That was a mouthful. And as concise as it gets.

Rodman had never angered the public like this before, and he slowly began to realize that his beloved persona was on the brink of extinction.

He agreed to an interview with Chris Wallace on ABC's "PrimeTime Live," but did nothing to quell the storm.

"It's sad that it has come to this," Rodman said. "It's a national crisis that I kicked a human being. I've lost a million dollars; I lost a couple hundred thousand dollars to an individual, and plus my reputation, which wasn't good in the first place, is just getting dragged all in quicksand . . . for no reason."

Rodman claimed that he didn't kick Amos in the groin, and that the kick was nothing more than a slight tap.

"If that's his groin, he's gotta be ... he's gotta be ... oh my God ... his wife must really love him," Rodman said.

And the interview was just getting started.

Wallace: Don't you take into account—pardon the expression—that you're a repeat offender?

Rodman: I am not a repeat offender. There is people in the league that trash-talk, do some things—

Wallace: But wait. You are a repeat offender. Ten suspensions over your career.

Rodman: For what? For what? Because some people lied to me in San Antonio? People did this to me and that to me, and what?

Wallace: You make it sound like you're the victim.

Rodman: The victim? No, I'm just showing the human side of the individual.

"I blame the narrow-minded, shallow people in the world . . . I mean the papers, the media. That's who I blame. You know, I did something that looked like it's bad. But on the other hand, it's harmless."

— Dennis Rodman

Wallace: Some people would say that's a little less on the human side.

Rodman: They won't get Dennis Rodman. I don't get paid nine million dollars a year just to go out there and look good. It's entertainment. I've got to give you the total package. If I can't give you that, I'm worthless.

And there you have it: a point-blank admission that everything about Rodman is contrived, carefully packaged and sold to you, the fans.

But instead of accepting responsibility, Rodman blamed the media for crucifying an easy target.

"I blame the narrow-minded, shallow people in the world. I mean the papers, the media," Rodman said. "That's who I blame. You know, I did something that looked like it's bad. But on the other hand, it's harmless. It's very harmless. It's the same thing that happened to me last year, head-butting an official. Everybody said, 'Screw him, screw him, I told you he would do it, he did it in San Antonio.'

"But when I won the championship, oh my God, they threw a parade. I jumped on everybody's shoulder, I'm God, I'm the savior, sign him back. Get him back to Chicago, we need him, we need him again. Now it's happening again."

Wallace, whose hard-nosed reporting was a tribute to his profession, read Stern's statement to Rodman.

Wallace: He says you have to persuade him it won't happen again.

Rodman: I don't say that. I cannot say that. If I'm on the court, there's no one else. It's just me and my intensity. I fight them, but I don't lash out at any other players. If it happens, it just means that I had a bad day.

Wallace: But if David Stern says to you, 'Dennis, can you promise me you won't have any more bad days?' What are you going to say?

Rodman: I'm gonna say, first of all, "Don't treat me like your

kid. I'm not your son, you're not my father." That's the first thing
we need to get straight.

Wallace then asked Rodman point-blank if he needed help.

"I don't need help," Rodman said. "I'm not crying out and lashing out to anybody. People have emotional problems, but that's part of life. That is part of life. Everyone who has problems don't need to go to the damn doctor. It's just part of life, experiencing what's going on.

"[People think] 'Oh, he's done it again, he's at it again. What's wrong with that psycho?' They don't understand, though, I'm not crazy. I know exactly what's going on."

> **Wallace:** Do you know exactly what's going on?
>
> **Rodman:** Oh, yeah. I know exactly what's going on.
>
> **Wallace:** Well, that raises the question. I'm not saying you did this for that reason, but isn't all of this . . . good for business?
>
> **Rodman:** Yeah. It's good for everything.

The controversy surrounding Rodman had become a national issue, and none other than President Clinton jumped into the fray, appealing to Rodman's sensibilities.

In an interview with a New York television station, Clinton told Rodman that it wasn't too late to turn the incident into a positive message.

"I'm a fan of Dennis Rodman," Clinton said. "I'm sure in his heart of hearts, he regrets [kicking the cameraman]. But I would hope that at some point in addition to paying this enormous fine, and also to pay the gentleman he kicked . . . that he'll find a way to say, 'I shouldn't have done it and I really regret it.'

"There are lots of kids out there like that—real smart, real able, a little bit different—and they've got to be fascinated by him, so

253

I'll hope he'll find a way to say that. . . . He might be able to help some young people if he just says. 'That's something I shouldn't have done. I'm not going to do that anymore.' "

While he ignored the unsolicited advice, Rodman reacted with joy to Clinton's remarks, impressed that his antics had landed the biggest fish in the attention pool.

"The president is a fan of Dennis Rodman," Rodman told the Chicago *Sun-Times* in an exclusive interview. "Man! It leaves me a little speechless. This is the greatest thing I could've expected."

RODMAN'S LIST OF SUSPENSIONS

DATE	TEAM	GAMES	REASON
Nov. 1992	Detroit	1	Missing training camp
Dec. 1992	Detroit	1	Missing practice
Dec. 1993	Detroit	1	Head-butting the Bulls' Stacey King
March 1994	San Antonio	1	Head-butting Utah's John Stockton
May 1994	San Antonio	1	Undercutting Utah's Tom Chambers and kneeing John Stockton.
Nov. 1994	San Antonio	1	Throwing bag of ice at coach Bob Hill during game
Dec. 1994	San Antonio	1	Missing practice
March 1996	Chicago	6	Head-butting a referee
Dec. 1996	Chicago	2	Profane tirade against NBA Commissioner David Stern and referees
Jan. 1997	Chicago	11	Kicking a cameraman

Clinton's involvement only fed the monster, and clearly, Rodman failed to realize what the furor was all about, and the answer was respect.

Rodman had shown the ultimate hypocrisy, continually ripping a new generation of players for lack of respect while kicking a civilian who was simply doing his job. And he had placed another black cloud over the Bulls organization, one that would linger for the rest of the season.

They would be faced with an unpalatable dilemma, and they would have to reexamine their priorities.

How much was it worth to win with Dennis Rodman?

Was it worth the integrity of an organization, one that had clawed for eight years to reach the pinnacle?

And where would they be in June?

Holding another championship trophy?

Or sitting at home, victimized by the enemy within, wondering if the great Rodman experiment had been worth the hassle?

Maybe the Bulls were getting what they paid for, buying the illusion that they could be the team to finally rehabilitate Dennis Rodman.

In that regard, there was only a sorry precedent.

Nevertheless, the playoffs were coming, and their legacy was on the line.

And once again, a team with Dennis Rodman was on the brink of disaster.

"I'm not Mother Teresa, and I'm not wearing a white robe everywhere I go," Rodman said. "And I have different sides to me that most people in this business don't have or they're just afraid to show.

"I'm different. I'm . . . I'm just too . . . just too Dennis Rodman."

Indeed, too much Dennis Rodman.

Too much for his own good.

Final Act

"I'm not changing. No way in hell."

Dennis Rodman

n every Dennis Rodman story, there is a cycle.

Boy is good, boy is loved, boy gets bored.

Boy is bad, boy is punished, boy rebels.

Boy comes back, boy succeeds, boy is forgiven.

Boys are always forgiven.

It is Rodman's blessing and his curse.

"Rodman needs to be ignored." Houston Rockets center Hakeem Olajuwon said. "But the media can't get enough of him. This is what young children see. They think that's cool. He's corrupting society and we're giving him the opportunity to do that. He's getting endorsements. It's disgusting."

Yet after his latest digression, Rodman would find himself testing the boundaries of tolerance like never before.

It wasn't the 11-game suspension, which turned out to be just another forgotten episode on Rodman's rap sheet.

After a prolonged stay in Las Vegas, Rodman finally met with NBA commissioner David Stern, who backed off his demand for psychiatric counseling.

And although Stern issued a strong warning that the next digression could be his last in the NBA, Rodman benefitted from a little spin control and a lot of good fortune.

After being reinstated, Rodman volunteered to play the next eleven games for free. His salary, roughly $109,000 per game, would be donated to eleven assorted charities. It was a transparent move to fall back in the good graces of Chicago fans, and it worked.

Then came a bit of redemption. Eugene Amos, the cameraman who gained $200,000 as a result of Rodman's temper, was arrested in Minneapolis, accused of assaulting his girlfriend. It turned out she had filed domestic abuse charges on January 14, the day before Amos's baseline encounter with Rodman.

And on the night of his return to the Bulls, Rodman once again became the object of sympathy. A tabloid television show had flown in Philander Rodman from the Philippines, where he would watch his son in person for the first time.

The TV show featured Philander walking the streets of Chicago like an awestruck tourist. They filmed him visiting his own father, who also lives in Chicago, but suffers from many health problems. And he was shown sitting in the United Center, chomping on popcorn while his estranged son went to work.

But there was no tearful reunion. There were no words spoken.

Very simply, Dennis Rodman wanted no part of a father he has never known.

"All of a sudden he wants to cash in on my fame," Rodman said. "It ain't happening."

What did happen was more significant. The presence of his father and his obvious motives had transformed Rodman from symbol of evil into an object of compassion, the child from a broken home who needed positive reinforcement.

And after his first game back with the Bulls, Rodman received an on-court hug from Michael Jordan, the biggest endorsement one could ever hope for in Chicago.

Shortly afterwards, Carl's Jr.—the restaurant chain that had pulled its national advertising campaign centered on Rodman—began running the commercials as if nothing happened. And Converse, which had just signed Rodman to a hefty contract to wear and endorse its shoes, announced that a television campaign had prompted the price of its stock to rise 37 percent.

Rodman had survived. For the moment.

"Young children love Dennis Rodman," said Dwight Manley, his agent. "Women, especially older women, love Dennis Rodman because they don't see the barriers that certain uptight males [project]. They see this pure, wonderful individual . . . this giving guy who is creative, who is fun, and little kids see the same thing.

"They don't see the stereotypes, and with Dennis, that's what they get."

Indeed, the stage was once again decorated for a triumphant ending. The playoffs were coming, the time when Rodman would turn up the intensity until his opponent no longer wanted to compete, the time when he would help lead the Bulls to another NBA championship, proving that all the nuisances and suspensions were worth the investment.

Except Dennis Rodman had run out of luck.

He would miss the last thirteen games of the regular season after suffering a knee injury. He would return in time for a first-round playoff battle against the Washington Bullets, but with a cumbersome brace wrapped around his knee, he was almost invisible on the court.

And things only got worse. During the series against the Bullets, Rodman's second book, *Walk on the Wild Side*, hit the market, one so tasteless and tawdry that it created a significant backlash.

After waxing about the sexual relationship of President Clinton and his wife and describing how one of his fantasies would involve tying up David Stern and painting him with lipstick, Oprah Winfrey cancelled Rodman's appearance on her show.

If only by coincidence, the referees began monitoring Rodman like never before. In the next series against the Atlanta Hawks, technical difficulties and constant foul trouble reduced Rodman to a cheerleader on the end of the bench. At one point, Rodman had a string of at least one technical in thirteen consecutive playoff games.

"It's become a comedy routine," Rodman said. "The refs are trying to get the best of me. I can't even step on the court without the referees blowing the whistle on me.

"I think I'm getting shafted. The whole world could see I'm being singled out."

Sensing he had gone too far, Rodman tried to distance himself from his latest book. He claimed the coauthor took great creative license in some areas, taking things and "tweaking them like he was on acid or mushrooms." He said the next time, he would write the book himself and "see if it sells."

It was almost as pathetic as Charles Barkley claiming to be misquoted in his own autobiography.

Yes, Rodman had become desperate. He was no longer a rebounding machine or the source of maniacal energy on the court. He was no longer a factor in the championship run, a time when he normally dominated.

During the NBA Finals, Rodman was a nonfactor, smothered by Utah Jazz forward Karl Malone. He did little to try and channel his energy to basketball, which infuriated his teammates the most.

He left his teammates twice to go and "relax" in Las Vegas. And on a Saturday night, just seventeen hours before Game 4, Rodman was holed up in a nightclub called The Holy Cow. According to a bar spokeswoman, a nasty incident almost materialized when one patron allegedly threw a cigarette at someone in Rodman's entourage.

"We can't control Dennis off the court," Scottie Pippen said. "You would think Dennis would want to start looking and evaluating what is going on on the court with himself."

And on a fateful afternoon in Salt Lake City, Rodman once again inserted foot in mouth.

He blamed his invisible act on a "lack of sex."

He said he needed to rent a bike, ride through the mountains, and "find God or somebody who could help him find Dennis Rodman."

And he said he had a hard time "getting in sync because of all the asshole Mormons."

The latter was possibly the dumbest thing Rodman had said since denouncing Larry Bird after the 1987 Eastern Conference Finals.

The Anti-Defamation League and the NAACP soon issued critical responses, stating that the Bulls and the NBA should not tolerate what amounts to religious persecution.

While Rodman tried to apologize, the NBA stuck him with a $50,000 fine.

And before Game 6, Rodman was grilled by NBC's Jim Gray

about his comment toward Mormons. Rodman broke down and began to cry, finally throwing his microphone down and storming out of the room.

Whether it was contrived or not, it stemmed from one realization, that Rodman may have burned his final bridge in Chicago.

"People are going to make sure that I won't come back here, and the league will make sure that I won't come back here," Rodman said. "If anything goes wrong in this organization, like anything else, it'll probably be on one guy. I'm the target guy.

"Like I said, they're trying to blackball me. If the league wants to force me out of this business, that's great. I took the money. I guess I'll have to run."

The Bulls would eventually win the championship on the sheer determination and brilliance of Michael Jordan and the maturity of Scottie Pippen. But Rodman was no longer the third wheel, dropped from the headline act.

And as they celebrated on the floor of the United Center, it was clear Rodman had become a bit player, much of it from his own doing.

For Rodman, the behavior was consistent with a litany of self-destruction. He will charm you, endear himself to all with his innocence and shyness, then break your heart for no apparent reason. No matter who you are, he will test your patience. It is as inevitable as the sun rising.

Maybe he can't deal with happiness. Maybe he can't get along with adults. Maybe he is damaged goods, destined to complete a life of self-inflicted punishment.

"I feel sorry for him," Utah Jazz president Frank Layden said. "I pray for him. And I'm not a Mormon, I'm a Catholic. Because I think what we are seeing is nothing but tragedy in that guy's life.

"I can't imagine the places he goes, the things he does. I think someday we'll pick up the paper and we are going to see: RODMAN DEAD. You can't live your life after midnight, hanging out with bad people. He's a life wasted."

If nothing else, Rodman may have finally worn out his welcome in Chicago, in the NBA, and in society.

Or maybe he has us all fooled.

While his future was once again in doubt, with Rodman, there is no other option. It is familiar footing.

For he could be living the charmed life of a cartoon character, the kind that gets flatted by a falling boulder, only to get up, wipe off the dust, and take off down the road.

And just hours after the Bulls attended a Grant Park rally honoring their fifth championship, Rodman showed up at the United Center for his World Championship Wrestling debut.

He jumped in the ring. He was strangled by The Giant, then thrown to the canvas when Hulk Hogan came to his rescue.

As The Giant turned his vengeance toward a new enemy, Rodman grabbed Hogan's title belt and cracked The Giant in the back of the head.

The Giant fell to the ground, soon to receive a few flying elbows from Rodman.

It is a metaphor for his life.

"I'm not a role model," Rodman said. "I'm a figment of your imagination. I'm a cartoon character you watch every so often. But you love to watch me.

"And if I'm so bad, why am I still here? Eleven years later, I'm still alive, still kicking."

After all, it takes a lot to kill off an antihero.

Especially one as bad as Dennis Rodman.